101
GANGSTER
MOVIES
YOU MUST SEE BEFORE YOU DIE

GENERAL EDITOR
STEVEN JAY SCHNEIDER

APPLE

ISBN: 9781845436056

This book was designed and produced by
Quintessence Editions Ltd.
The Old Brewery, 6 Blundell Street
London, N7 9BH

www.1001beforeyoudie.com

Update Editor	Elspeth Beidas
Update Designer	Isabel Eeles
Project Editor	Chrissy Williams
Editor	James Harrison
Editorial Assistant	Helena Baser
Designer	Howard Sherwood
Editorial Director	Jane Laing
Publisher	Mark Fletcher

The moral right of the contributors of this Work has been asserted
in accordance with the Copyright, Designs and Patents Act of 1988

Colour reproduction by Pica Digital Pte Ltd., Singapore.
Printed and bound in China.

9 8 7 6 5 4 3 2 1

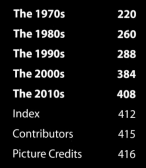

CONTENTS

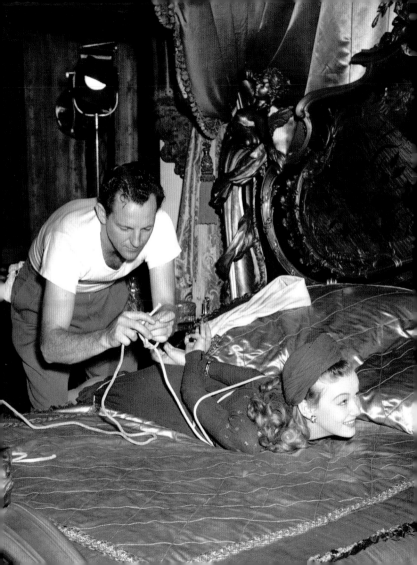

INTRODUCTION Steven Jay Schneider, General Editor

Movies about gangsters and their antitheses—cops, private eyes, and special agents—have been around since the pioneering days of cinema (*The Musketeers of Pig Alley* [1912]). Despite being a predominantly American genre, there have been many memorable entries from countries around the globe, including England (*Sexy Beast* [2000]), France (*Pépé le Moko* [1937]), Germany (*Short Sharp Shock* [1998]), Japan (*Branded to Kill* [1967]), and Hong Kong (*Hard-Boiled* [1992]). And within the U.S., gangster films have been given specific treatment within the African-American community (*Boyz N the Hood* [1991]), the Hispanic community (*Carlito's Way* [1993]), and the immigrant community (*Eastern Promises* [2007]).

Why are gangster movies so popular? Here are five reasons:

1. **Dynamic anti-heroes.** Who could forget Tony Montana (Al Pacino), "Rico" Bandello (Edward G. Robinson), "Cody" Jarrett (James Cagney), or Bonnie and Clyde (Faye Dunaway and Warren Beatty)?

2. **Colorful supporting roles.** Think Tommy DeVito (Joe Pesci) and you get the picture.

3. **Dramatic action.** Just recall the opening scene in *Gangs of New York* (2002), the car chase in *The French Connection* (1971), or any scene in *Reservoir Dogs* (1992).

4. **Gritty urban locales.** The tenements, alleyways, penthouses . . . crime lurks on every corner. In no other genre is location so crucial to the storytelling.

5. **Director magnets.** Hawks; Walsh; Lang; Malle; Coppola; Scorsese; Leone; Woo; Mann; Tarantino. Great directors are so often at their greatest in this genre.

Steven J. Schneider

Hollywood, U.S.A.

THE SCREENS FIRST GANGSTER FILM

D. W. GRIFFITH'S
The Musketeers
of Pig Alley

STARRING

LILLIAN
GISH

ELMER
BOOTH

HARRY
CAREY

WALTER
MILLER

ALFRED
PAGET

THE MUSKETEERS OF PIG ALLEY
1912 (U.S.)

Director D. W. Griffith **Producer** Biograph Studios **Screenplay** D. W. Griffith, Anita Loos **Cinematography** G.W. Bitzer **Cast** Elmer Booth, Lilian Gish, Clara T. Bracy, Walter Miller, Alfred Paget, John T. Dillon, Madge Kirby, Harry Carey, Robert Harron, Spike Robinson, Adolph Lestina, Jack Pickford, Gertrude Bambrick

This sixteen-minute silent film by D. W. Griffith is widely credited as the first gangster movie ever made. It was apparently influenced by the attention paid by the nationwide press to the murder of gambler Herman Rosenthal, and the high-profile trials and police scandals that resulted. Griffith was sufficiently intrigued by this true-life crime story to take his camera to the Lower East Side, and he cast actual street hoods and gangsters from the neighborhood as extras to authenticate his footage. Although the resulting film has very little to do with the Rosenthal case, it was the first time the Lower East Side was used as the central backdrop in a motion picture. It thus provides a fascinating window into the past.

The film's episodic plot centers on a poor married couple living in New York. The husband (Miller) works as a musician and must travel frequently for work. During one of his trips away from home, he is robbed by The Snapper Kid (Booth), chief of the Musketeers gang. Later, the musician gets caught up in a shootout and recognizes one of the gangsters as The Snapper Kid. Now he decides he wants his money back.

◄
The poster boldly makes the claim that this is the first gangster film. G. W. "Billy" Bitzer shot this and nearly all Griffith's subsequent films.

Griffith clearly saw The Snapper Kid sympathetically; Booth portrays him as a likeable, tough, coarse thief and killer. Not unlike the iconic gangsters soon to be played by James Cagney, The Snapper Kid is short, powerful, explosive, and expressive with his body, face, and gestures. He is violent and quick to react with movements that snap forth like his name. He is sly enough to avoid going to jail, wise enough not to fight in the

"ONE OF THE MOST VIVID PICTURES OF TENEMENT LIFE THAT THE EARLY AMERICAN CINEMA PRODUCED." PHIL HARDY

wrong places, and is constantly putting plans into action to get what he wants. He exudes a healthy self-confidence and is proud of the sharp way he dresses. Griffith's blending of realistic detail and romantic bias actually shaded the Chief of the Musketeers as more chivalrous than subsequent movie gangsters, but The Snapper Kid launched the central figure of the genre—the sympathetic gangster—and those who have come since share many of his traits.

► Lilian Gish plays "The Little Lady" who gets caught up with gangster life. The gangster genre began in the slums, and the people who lived there must have appreciated this film enormously.

The Lower East Side locale also provided an appropriate setting for the birth of the genre. "New York's other side" as a title card describes it, is made up of dingy rooms and hallways, saloons, narrow streets teeming with immigrants, and underworld alleyways filled with garbage cans, dust, and debris. City textures and dark spaces predominate. We are placed around the bottoms of buildings, and we never see the sky. **ER**

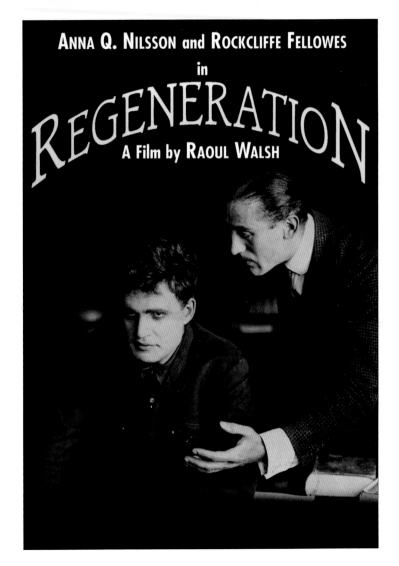

REGENERATION 1915 (U.S.)

Director Raoul Walsh **Screenplay** Raoul Walsh, Carl Harbaugh, Owen Frawley Kildare (based on autobiography, *My Mamie Rose*), Walter C. Hackett and Kildare (uncredited play, *The Regeneration*) **Cinematography** Georges Benoît **Cast** John McCann, James A. Marcus, Maggie Weston, Rockliffe Fellowes, Anna Nilsson, Carl Harbaugh

Filmed on location in New York's infamous Bowery district—which was apparently just as seedy in 1915 as it is today—Raoul Walsh's gangster drama and social document *Regeneration* is notable for its surprisingly realistic performances and plethora of impressive camera angles (including the giddy shot of a man falling from a fourth-story window). Walsh's first film after he left D. W. Griffith's company, and his first important directorial effort, it puts a grim spotlight on the rougher side of life in old New York. Adapted from the autobiography of turn-of-the-century gangster Owen Frawley Kildare, it is justifiably revered as a seminal silent film for its emphasis on character and milieu.

A young Irish-American "child of the slums," named Owen Conway (McCann), is adopted by an elderly neighbor couple who immediately put the boy to work. Their drunken fighting constitutes the only home he knows. He quickly escapes and grows up on the streets, where he learns to do whatever it takes to survive. By the time he has reached the ripe old age of twenty-five, Owen has become a ruthless gang leader. Owen's story runs parallel to that of Maire "Mamie Rose" Deering (Nilsson), a high-society lady who abandons her life of luxury to

◀

With its remarkably realistic acting, fast pace, and robust violent action, *Regeneration* set a new standard for silent films.

become a settlement worker in New York's slum district. Mamie takes it upon herself to teach the surly gangster how to read and write, and he soon begins to realize that he's been living his life the wrong way. Complicating his road to redemption—or rather, "regeneration"—is the fact that the city's crusading district attorney (Harbaugh) is not only Owen's bitterest enemy, but his bitterest rival for Mamie's affections.

"THE FIRST FEATURE-LENGTH GANGSTER MOVIE EVER MADE."

ATTRIBUTED TO RAOUL WALSH (DIRECTOR)

Although the plot is fairly conventional, the atmosphere really elevates things: the colorful characters, the teeming tenement (especially as seen on sidewalks and in the streets), the sense of an environment that has such a detrimental impact on human lives. *Regeneration* ultimately espouses a theory popular with social reformers of the time, namely that criminals are good people who are merely the product of their environment. And so the dramatic tension here can be summarized as follows: although Owen has the potential to be reformed by love, will he be able to resist the pull of his former life?

Walsh's innovative direction and brilliant use of cross-cutting set the standard for the dynamic visual language that would come to be identified as synonymous with the gangster genre in subsequent decades. *Regeneration* is undeniably one of the few classics of pre-1920 American cinema. **KW**

► **Rockcliffe Fellowes with a distinctive eye patch for added menace plays the gang leader torn between his gang and his moll.**

DR. MABUSE, THE GAMBLER
1922 (GERMANY)

Director Fritz Lang **Producer** Erich Pommer **Screenplay** Fritz Lang, Thea von Harbou (from a novel by Norbert Jacques) **Cinematography** Carl Hoffmann **Music** Konrad Elfers **Cast** Rudolf Klein-Rogge, Aud Egede Nissen, Alfred Abel, Gertrude Welker, Lil Dagover, Paul Richter, Bernhard Goetzke, Julius Herrmann

Fritz Lang's masterful *Dr. Mabuse, the Gambler* (a.k.a. *Dr. Mabuse, der Spieler*) is more than just a gangster film. For one thing, it was initially *two* gangster films. It was released in two feature-length parts: *Part 1: The Great Gambler—A Picture of Our Times* in April 1922, and *Part 2: Inferno—A Game of People of Our Time* in May 1922. Put together, these parts form a monumental almost-five-hour whole that is one of the towering achievements not just of 1920s German cinema but of 1920s cinema generally.

The film presents the many plots and plans of master criminal Mabuse (Klein-Rogge) in his ongoing conflict with his nemesis, State Prosecutor Wenk (Goetzke). In doing this, *Dr. Mabuse, the Gambler* helps to establish some of the key conventions adopted by later gangster movies—among them, the violent public elimination of witnesses, murderous urban shoot-outs, and a narrative organized around the rise and fall of the gangster. As the references to "our times" in the titles of both its parts suggest, *Dr. Mabuse* also presents a picture of the milieu, one particularly sensitive to the city's decadent delights—for example, "Cards or cocaine" is a nightclub

◄
The movie that launched the character of Dr. Mabuse. He appeared again in *The Testament of Dr. Mabuse* **and** *The 1000 Eyes of Dr. Mabuse.*

greeting heard in the film—as well as its alienating qualities. Dr. Mabuse himself is clearly an expression of urban modernity. He is associated with technology—the film begins with his overseeing a complicated robbery via the telephone—and he is also a master of disguise who easily blends into the anonymity of the city. Early on we see him shuffling photographs of his various disguises and, as the narrative proceeds, he shows up in

"I FEEL LIKE A STATE WITHIN THE STATE. COME AND GET ME!"

DR. MABUSE

a wide range of locations and in all sections of a divided society. The problem for Mabuse is that a man with many identities can ultimately become a man with no identity of his own, and *Dr. Mabuse* concludes with Mabuse's descent into madness as his crimes finally overwhelm him. By contrast, his adversary Wenk is also not averse to donning disguises but always retains a sense of his own self.

It is hard to keep a good super-villain down, however, and the character of Mabuse returned in Lang's *The Testament of Dr. Mabuse* (1933) and *The Thousand Eyes of Dr. Mabuse* (1960), as well as showing up as a stock villain in a series of 1960s German thrillers. He has also been seen as a template for later James Bond villains. More alarmingly, some cultural historians have found intimations of Hitler in Mabuse's hypnotic gaze and his uncanny ability to bend people to his will. **PH**

▶

Alfred Abel with Rudolf Klein-Roger as Dr. Mabuse, a model early 20th century villain with staying power.

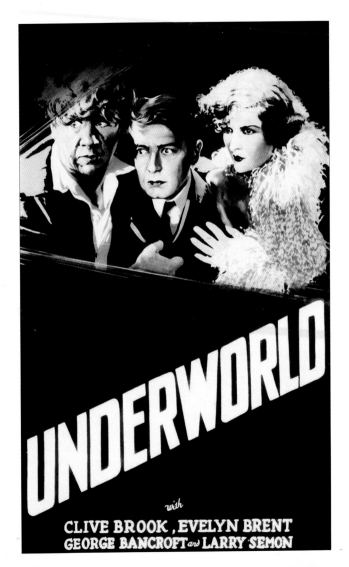

UNDERWORLD 1927 (U.S.)

Director Josef von Sternberg **Producers** B. P. Schulberg, Hector Turnbull
Screenplay Ben Hecht, Charles Furthman, Robert N. Lee **Cinematography** Bert
Glennon **Cast** George Bancroft, Evelyn Brent, Clive Brook, Fred Kohler, Helen Lynch,
Larry Semon, Jerry Mandy, Alfred Allen, Shep Houghton, Karl Morse, Julian Rivero

Such was the impact of *The Blue Angel* (1930), the film that
brought Marlene Dietrich to Hollywood, that it is easy to forget
that director Josef von Sternberg had already directed several
Hollywood movies. *The Salvation Hunters* (1925), his feature
debut, had so impressed Charlie Chaplin that he hired Sternberg
to make *The Sea Gull* (1926). But it was the vividly poetic
melodrama *Underworld* (1927) that propelled Sternberg, and it
is often cited as the first true Hollywood gangster film.

Underworld carries Sternberg's unmistakeable stamp,
particularly after the halfway mark as plot gives way to mood.
Sternberg explained: "When I made *Underworld* I was not a
gangster, nor did I know anything about gangsters . . . I don't
value the fetish for authenticity. On the contrary, the illusion of
reality is what I look for, not reality itself."

Where the film differs most from later variations is in von
Sternberg's typical concentration on the rivalries, intrigues, and
sexual jealousies within the gangster hierarchy, with little
attention given to the relationship between the criminals and
law enforcers. Stylistically, it contains a number of bravura
sequences, most famously the gangsters' ball—a seething

◄
**The first film
to adopt the
perspective
of the gangster,
Underworld was
internationally
influential,
particularly on the
pessimistic French
school of the 1930s.**

maelstrom of frenzied activity, distorted angles, and rapid, grotesque close-ups, ably conveying the title card's description of a "devil's carnival" set to "the brutal din of cheap music, booze, hate, and lust."

Much of the trajectory and trappings of the classical gangster movie is to be found here. The dialogue is slangy and pithy (conveyed, of course, in title cards), and there is a stirringly

"THERE WERE NO LIES IN IT, EXCEPT FOR A HALF-DOZEN SENTIMENTAL TOUCHES INTRODUCED BY THE DIRECTOR." *HECHT*

violent climax. Writer Ben Hecht, the former Chicago newsman whose list of future screenwriting credits included *Scarface* (1932), is chiefly responsible for establishing the picture's groundbreaking sense of authenticity, having noted as a crime reporter that "nice people . . . loved criminals." His principal innovation was "to skip the heroes and heroines [and] write a movie containing only villains and bawds."

So radical did the movie seem at first, with its complete immersion in the strange and unhealthy world of the professional criminal, that Paramount anticipated a box-office disaster. In the event, Hecht's basic instinct—that nice people love criminals—proved entirely correct for the gangster genre. A neon sign glimpsed in the film reading "The World Is Yours" anticipates not merely Hecht's later *Scarface*, but the imminent supremacy of the American screen gangster himself. **MC**

► Larry Sermon casts a suspicious glance as "Slippy" Lewis— another of the *Underworld* criminals.

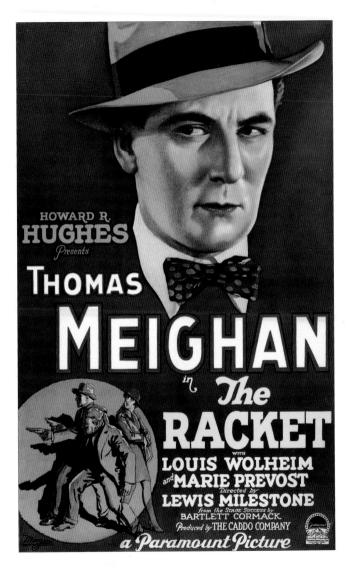

THE RACKET 1928 (U.S.)

Director Lewis Milestone **Producer** Howard Hughes **Writers** Bartlett Cormack (based on his play), Del Andrews, Harry Behn, Tom Miranda (titles) **Cinematography** Tony Gaudio **Music** Robert Israel **Cast** Thomas Meighan, Louis Wolheim, Marie Prevost, G. Pat Collins, Henry Sedley, George E. Stone, Sam De Grasse

Based on the hit Broadway play by *Chicago Daily News* reporter Bartlett Cormack, *The Racket* was nominated for the first-ever Best Picture Academy Award, losing out to *Wings* (1927). Directed by Lewis Milestone (*All Quiet on the Western Front* [1930]), this silent classic offers a thinly disguised portrait of a corrupt city government and a police force firmly in the pocket of a mobster who was clearly inspired by Al Capone. The mob leader is named Nick Scarsi (Wolheim), not far removed from Capone's nickname of "Scarface;" Chicago's mayor Big Bill Thompson here becomes "The Old Man," (McIntosh). Perhaps not surprisingly given the sensitivities of the Prohibition and gangster–rackeeting era both the play and the film were banned in Chicago.

Thomas Meighan plays James McQuigg, a police captain at an imaginary downtown precinct. McQuigg devotes himself to ridding the city of the influence of gangsters, especially Scarsi. The two have a grudging admiration for each other although the mob boss uses this primarily to distract and taunt the captain. Scarsi invites McQuigg to his brother Joe's (Stone's) birthday party. Both men are readily aware that

◄

The Howard Hughes silent version is said to have sparked Hollywood's gangster cycle. It also prompted a less successful 1951 remake with Robert Ryan and Robert Mitchum.

McQuigg's actions are only tolerated when they don't interfere with the criminal network that runs the city (and that extends as high as the mayor). When McQuigg gets too zealous in his pursuit of Scarsi, he is reassigned to a remote precinct. He still means to bring down the crime boss, however, and the last section of the movie deals with his efforts to goad Scarsi into one last showdown.

"I'D LIKE [TO] SLEEP BUT BY THE TIME I GET THROUGH WITH THE CORONER IT'LL BE TIME TO GO TO MASS." MCQUIGG

In the end, *The Racket* is pretty much your standard cops-versus-gangsters movie. It is perhaps most laudable for the easy entertainment it offers. This is, above all, a solid, well-made, late silent-era film. It has enough action and comedy to keep things moving at a brisk pace; and the actors are all more than competent. Perhaps most important for posterity, the performances are largely devoid of the hammy overacting common to many silent films; on the whole, the actors here portray their characters using a relatively naturalistic style.

► **Marie Prevost plays Helen Hayes, a nightclub singer, gold digger, and way in for police Captain McQuigg (Meighan) to bring down Scarsi.**

Adding to its legend, *The Racket* was believed to be lost until it was discovered in the collection of billionaire recluse Howard Hughes, who produced it. As both a gangster film and a political exposé, it is ultimately an interesting curio that gripped audiences during cinema's early years. It certainly held its own against a "talkie" version made in 1951. **KW**

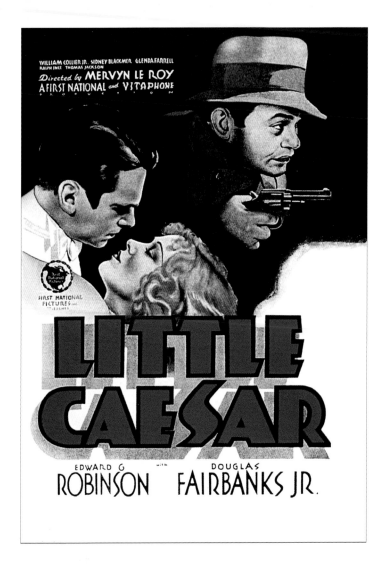

LITTLE CAESAR 1931 (U.S.)

Director Mervyn Le Roy **Producer** Hal Wallis, Darryl Zanuck **Screenplay** Francis Faragoh (from W. R. Burnett's novel) **Cinematography** Tony Gaudio **Music** Erno Rapee **Cast** Edward G. Robinson, Douglas Fairbanks Jr., Glenda Farrell, William Collier Jr., Sidney Blackmer, Ralph Ince, Thomas Jackson, Stanley Fields, Maurice Black

Released a few months before *The Public Enemy*, *Little Caesar* stands in film history as "officially" the first gangster movie. Based very loosely on the novel by W. R. Burnett, the picture lays down the basic template for all later mobster flicks.

Rico Bandello (Robinson) is an up-and-coming hoodlum on the streets of an unnamed American city. From an ideological perspective, the anonymous city (is it Chicago? New York? Kansas City?) is significant, since the social warning inherent in the film about the dangers of the criminal underworld is applicable to *all* cities, and not just New York or Chicago. The story charts Rico's rise to power, ultimately dominating the underworld, until his downfall and finally his death at the wrong end of a tommy gun.

Little Caesar not only created the anti–rags-to-riches, dark side of the American Dream motif of the gangster genre, but also introduced a whole new language to American cinema. This was the film that popularized such now-clichéd gangster-speak as "gats" (guns), "molls" (girls), and "bulls" (cops). Although this language may (or may not) have been popular on the mean streets of the mobsters' own cities, it was the popularity

◄

Rico Caesar is represented as a vicious and ruthlessly ambitious mobster in arguably one of the most influential movies of the gangster genre.

of *Little Caesar* that brought this parlance to the popular screen. As a movie, *Little Caesar* is typical of early sound cinema: the cinematography is largely static and most of the performances are overly melodramatic, but it is Robinson's central performance as Rico that is absolutely electrifying, even today. It is now a Hollywood legend, but, ironically, the reason Robinson closes his eyes when he fires his gun is because the very gentle

"MOTHER OF MERCY! IS THIS THE END OF RICO?"

RICO BANDELLO

Edward G. always jumped when guns went off, even those he was firing. Despite being appalled by the genre of violence, Robinson found himself largely typecast in subsequent films— he was never properly allowed to let Rico die in his career.

The film's opening credits are superimposed over Burnett's novel, thereby calling attention to the literary origin of the story and (perhaps more important) distancing the portrayal of Rico from any real, and currently active, mobster like Al Capone. The word "Prohibition," which was still the law at the time, is never actually spoken, nor is bootlegging depicted as it would be in *The Public Enemy* and *Scarface* (1932). This was probably because of the Production Code, which had just come into effect and prohibited the depiction of real crime or criminal activity on celluloid. Be that as it may, *Little Caesar* was still banned in certain Canadian provinces for glorifying criminals. **MK**

► Edward G. Robinson (born Emmanual Goldenberg) became a box office star thanks to his vicious portrayal of Caesar Enrico Bandello, clearly based on Al Capone.

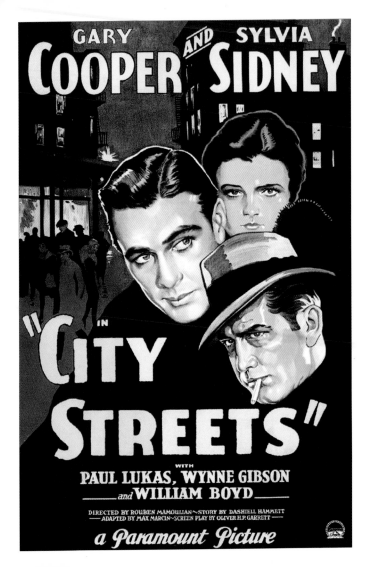

CITY STREETS 1931 (U.S.)

Director Rouben Mamoulian **Producer** E. Lloyd Sheldon **Screenplay** Max Marcin, Oliver H. P. Garrett, based on a story by Dashiell Hammett **Cinematography** Lee Garmes **Music** Sidney Cutner **Cast** Sylvia Sidney, Gary Cooper, Paul Lukas, Guy Kibbee, William Boyd, Wynne Gibson, Stanley Fields, Betty Sinclair, Robert Homans

City Streets was the second Hollywood project of Rouben Mamoulian, the maverick genius of talking cinema. Mamoulian would go on to direct such innovative masterpieces as *Dr. Jekyll and Mr. Hyde* (1931), *Love Me Tonight* (1932), and *Becky Sharp* (1935). Like his first film, the musical *Applause* (1929), *City Streets* sets its narrative against vibrantly used real locations, making use of unconventional angles and strikingly unusual—at times poetic—imagery, showing again that the supposed technological limitations of early sound cinema needed only imagination and skill to be overcome. The movie is also famous for inventing the cinematic convention of the voice-over, used by Mamoulian against the objections of the studio, who apparently feared audiences would be confused by the sound of disembodied voices.

The only story *The Maltese Falcon* author Dashiell Hammett conceived expressly for the screen, *City Streets* stars an excellent Sylvia Sidney (replacing Clara Bow after a much-publicized nervous breakdown) and a young Gary Cooper as lovers, whose relationship is cut short when she is caught carrying the gun used by her stepfather to kill a rival bootlegger. In prison she

◄
Director Mamoulian took a more stylized, arthouse approach to gangland melodrama with this release.

comes to reject the values of the criminal lifestyle she had previously urged Cooper to take up, and on release is horrified to discover that he has become henchman to "the Big Fella"— the lecherous head of the bootlegging organization.

Though ultimately respectful of conventional morality, the picture features a number of instances of crimes going unpunished (which was impossible after the enforcement of

"WHEN YOU TALK TO ME, TAKE THAT TOOTHPICK OUTTA YOUR MOUTH."

THE KID

the Production Code in 1934) and is among the most cynical of the early gangster films in its total disenchantment with city living, which it portrays as almost inevitably corrupting.

None of the gangsters are especially unpleasant as people, and some, such as Guy Kibbee's jovial portrayal of Pop, are downright likeable. It is not the basically ordinary individuals drawn to this world but only their trade, presented by Mamoulian as a fact of urban life to be avoided rather than resisted, that is repugnant. With all of its killings kept off-screen (conveyed through symbolic devices such as a shot of the victim's hat floating along the river), *City Streets* is easily the most restrained of the first gangster talkies. Despite this more poetic approach, or perhaps because of it, the film was apparently considered the best of the bunch by no less an authority than real-life mobster Al Capone himself. **MC**

► Criminal henchman Gary Cooper and gangster's daughter Sylvia Sidney share an intimate, lighthearted moment as lovers.

THE PUBLIC ENEMY 1931 (U.S.)

Director William A. Wellman **Producer** Darryl F. Zanuck **Screenplay** John Bright, Kubec Glasmon, Harvey Thew **Cinematography** Dev Jennings **Editor** Edward M. McDermott **Cast** James Cagney, Edward Woods, Jean Harlow, Joan Blondell, Mae Clarke, Donald Cook, Leslie Fenton, Beryl Mercer, Robert O'Connor, Murray Kinnell

Edward G. Robinson in *Little Caesar* (1931) and Paul Muni in *Scarface* (1932) were magnetic but also repellent; it was James Cagney's Tom Powers in *The Public Enemy* that really set the gangster film on a collision course with conventional morality. From his first appearance in the opening credits, smiling at the audience and throwing a playful mock punch, it is obvious that this is a character with whom we are invited to identify. Cagney's personal charm and attractiveness are going to be fully utilized to help that process along. Of course, he will fall in the end ("I ain't so tough," he splutters in a singularly unconvincing censor-appeasing epiphany), but the preceding 80 minutes revel in his exploits with neither distance nor comment.

We see Powers' unhappy childhood and are encouraged to sympathize, then to share the excitement of his swift ascent through the underworld. We are every bit as seduced by his charm and sexual confidence as the women he accumulates (in the same spirit as he acquires the finest clothes, cars, and other luxuries). More than any other gangster of the early talking cinema, Powers invites vicarious identification in the audience. And yet, at the same time, he is a ruthless thug given to sudden

◄
Warner Bros. notched up notable successes with their gangster-versus-society movies in the 1930s. The careers of James Cagney and Jean Harlow were launched by this movie.

and unpredictable violence motivated by a child's sense of reasoning, as when he cold-bloodedly shoots the horse that threw and killed his friend, or viciously slams a grapefruit into the face of his girlfriend (Mae Clarke, who is, incredibly, uncredited) for the audacity of suggesting he not get drunk before breakfast. The film is the cruelest, most unpredictable of the first gangster talkies; fresh audiences can still be counted

"SO STRONG AS TO BE REPULSIVE IN SOME ASPECTS, PLUS A REVOLTING CLIMAX." VARIETY

upon to draw audible breath at the grotesque ending, with Powers' trussed-up, bullet-ridden corpse deposited upright on his mother's doorstep, falling in as the door opens and landing facedown with a sickening thud.

Remarkably, Cagney was originally cast in the role of "the good guy" played by Edward Woods, and some scenes were even shot with this casting in place. There are a variety of different accounts to explain why the switch was made. Director William Wellman claimed that it was his idea, whereas others insist that Woods himself made the request. Cagney himself certainly alluded to it, and either way, it is obvious that the actor knows this is going to be his breakthrough role, attacking it with an energy and ferocity that remain terrifying. Seizing her own big chance, Jean Harlow also stands out, fresh from *Hell's Angels* (1930), after two years of bit parts and walk-ons. **MC**

► **James Cagney crouches over his former bootlegging buddy's (Edward Woods) dead body in this iconic urban crime film.**

SCARFACE: THE SHAME OF A NATION 1932 (U.S.)

Director Howard Hawks, Richard Rosson (co-director) **Producers** Howard Hawks and Howard Hughes **Screenplay** Ben Hecht, Howard Hawks (uncredited) **Cinematography** Lee Garmes, L. W. O'Connell **Cast** Paul Muni, Ann Dvorak, Karen Morley, George Raft, Boris Karloff, Osgood Perkins, C. Henry Gordon, Vince Barnett

Obviously based upon the career of Al Capone (a fact screenwriter Ben Hecht was obliged to deny when he allegedly received a visit from some of Capone's men during production), *Scarface* traces the rise and fall of gangster Tony "Scarface" Camonte (Muni) calmly killing his way to power. Alongside the same year's criminally neglected *The Beast of the City*, *Scarface* sensationally completed the first wave of gangster films alongside *Little Caesar* and *The Public Enemy* (both 1931).

It differs in style from the latter two films, principally in that it was made for United Artists rather than Warner Bros. (though Muni, Raft, and Dvorak were all signed to Warners contracts), but in many ways it feels the most authentic, thanks in large part to Hecht, hot from the Chicago newsrooms (immortalized in his hit play *The Front Page*) and already possessed of Hollywood's best ear for naturalistic, slangy street dialogue. The cast is fine, too, with Muni in his star-making role (but unlike Cagney and Robinson, not genre-limiting), Raft as coin-flipping hood Rinaldo, and Dvorak sensational as Camonte's sister, in

◄

The theme of *Scarface* was gangsters as excited children playing deadly games. The final tally was 28 deaths, despite the censors having cut several scenes.

one of those intense, ballsy performances. Fascinating, too, is Boris Karloff, not yet a horror genre icon, as a soft-spoken gang boss who meets a brilliantly directed end in a bowling alley.

The censors objected to the violence, of course, and scenes had to be cut as a result. But Hawks directs the actual killings with a poetic reticence we may not have expected of him. More than this there was the problem of the film's entire tone,

"WE'LL LICK THEM ALL. THE NORTH SIDE, THE SOUTH SIDE. WE'LL LICK THE WHOLE WORLD." CAMONTE

which showed crime as an integral part of an exciting world of nightclubs, sex, and jazz, where dishonesty is openly rewarded and only occasionally punished. (Then there was Camonte's implicitly incestuous relationship with his sister—understated maybe, but by no means imagined.)

Various cosmetic efforts were made to soften the message, notably the subtitle "Shame of a Nation," and an opening rolling caption that cheekily claims the film is "an indictment of gang rule in America and of the callous indifference of the government." Commercial over, and *Scarface* is off, in a 95-minute blizzard of sensation that never lets up or catches its breath until the stunning finale, with Scarface's symbolic death beneath a Cook's Tours sign reading "The World Is Yours" (the sign was first seen in *Underworld* [1927])—one of the few points it has in common with Brian De Palma's remake in 1983. **MC**

► Paul Muni as brutal hoodlum Tony Camonte is about to pump lead into his rivals. It was the first crime film to show a gangster using a machine gun as weapon of choice.

THE TESTAMENT OF DR. MABUSE
1933 (GERMANY)

Director Fritz Lang **Producer** Seymour Nebenzal **Screenplay** Fritz Lang, Thea von Harbou **Cinematography** Fritz Arno Wagner (edited by Lothar Wolff with art direction by Karl Vollbrecht and Emil Hassler) **Music** Hans Erdmann **Music** Hans Erdmann **Cast** Rudolf Klein-Rogge, Otto Wernicke, Oscar Beregi, Karl Meixner

Back in 1922, Fritz Lang first introduced the pulp fictional master criminal Dr. Mabuse in a two-part, five-hour film. Returning to his character, against an implicit but easily identifiable background of the rise to power of the Nazis, Lang fully exploits the social and political symbolism of "the gangster." The film (a.k.a. *Das Testament des Dr. Mabuse*) also develops the first Mabuse notion, via framing and the camera, about the nature of cinematic images on spectators.

Mabuse (Klein-Rogge), now insane, is incarcerated in an asylum run by psychiatrist Professor Baum (Beregi). He spends his time writing endless pages on how to commit a series of seemingly meaningless and unconnected crimes. This will trigger off a general panic that can be exploited to seize power. It is here that the film's attack on the criminal nature of Nazism becomes clear. The way Lang represents the various gangsters working for an anonymous and faceless leader not only insists on their status as hoodlums ready to commit murder on command, but also highlights the way people can be led to abandon all capacity for thought and individual action to an

◄

The poster seems to reflect the darker political nature of this "criminal mind" movie, Lang's sequel to his *Dr. Mabuse, the Gambler.*

authoritarian figure. Baum's fascination with Mabuse has led to him being manipulated by Mabuse's exceptional mental capacities, a way of denouncing Nazi propaganda and mass mind control (think of newsreel footage of Germans leaping to their feet and shouting "Sieg Heil!" in unison). The brilliance of the film lies, however, in how Lang represents the strategies by which Baum (who turns out to be the leader of the gang) gives

"SLOGANS OF THE THIRD REICH HAVE BEEN PUT INTO THE MOUTHS OF CRIMINALS IN THE FILM." *LANG*

out instructions to his underlings. Whereas they assume their boss is seated behind a curtain as he gives them orders, they are in fact listening to a recording. This is a variation on the opening sequence where a monotonous, mechanical sound becomes unsettling by virtue of all lack of source. The spectator feels as threatened as the character hiding from the gangsters. Baum is always out of the frame when giving orders and is represented on screen by his voice, which is a metaphor for the way Lang manipulates the soundtrack from an unseen vantage point outside the range of the camera. Both Lang and Baum pull strings off screen. Similarly, by showing a ghost-like image exiting Mabuse's dead body and entering that of Baum, Lang introduces the theme of vision and raises the question of the very status of the cinematic image and the fascination it exerts on the spectator. **RH**

► Rudolf Klein-Rogge as the criminally insane Dr. Mabuse running his empire of villains— perhaps, or perhaps not, an allegory of the Nazi Party.

MANHATTAN MELODRAMA 1933 (U.S.)

Directors W. S. Van Dyke, George Cukor (uncredited) **Producer** David
O. Selznick **Screenplay** Arthur Caesar, Oliver H. P. Garrett, Joseph L. Mankiewicz
Cinematography James Wong Howe **Cast** Myrna Loy, William Powell, Clark Gable,
George Sidney, Leo Carrillo, Nat Pendleton, Sabel Jewell, Muriel Evans

W. S. Van Dyke's *Manhattan Melodrama* has a real-life crime
connection. It is the film John Dillinger, a huge Myrna Loy fan,
supposedly came out of hiding to see when he was gunned
down by federal agents.

The movie is aptly named, as it is a melodrama of grand
proportions. The plot revolves around the lives of two
orphaned boys, Jim Wade (Powell) and Edward "Blackie"
Gallagher (played by Gable as a grown-up, with Mickey Rooney
acting Blackie as a kid). Though not related, Jim and Blackie are
raised as brothers by the kindly Poppa Rosen (Sidney). When
their adopted father is trampled by a police officer's horse
during a political rally, Blackie's already palpable anger and
resentment toward the law increases. As adults, Blackie makes
his living in illegal business pursuits, and Jim has become an
assistant district attorney. Blackie is the affable gangster as
only Gable is able to play him, ready to put his life on the line if
necessary to help his boyhood "brother." As each man climbs
the ladders of their respective businesses, they continue to
love and esteem each other, even after Blackie's girlfriend,
Eleanor Packer (Loy), leaves Blackie and consequently marries

◄

A proto-"buddy"
movie and
melodrama as
much as a gangster
film, "bad guy"
Gable and his
former friend from
the slums, now
D. A. Powell,
compete for the
affections of Loy.

Jim. So tight, in fact, is the bond between these two radically different men that each one risks his own life and livelihood for each other. For example, when Blackie is involved in the murder of a man who owes him money, Jim, now the district attorney, readily believes the evidence that Blackie fabricates in order to exonerate himself. In turn, when Blackie learns from Eleanor that Jim's career ambitions may be ruined, Blackie

"I'LL CLEAN OUT EVERY ROTTEN SPOT IN THIS CITY, AND, BLACKIE, I DON'T WANT TO FIND YOU IN ANY OF THEM!" WADE

commits an additional murder to cover up his deceit of Jim. The resulting tragedy ultimately threatens both men's happiness, careers, and, for one of them, his very life. The on-screen chemistry between Loy and Powell was such that they shared the billing in more than a dozen subsequent motion pictures, the most famous of which are the *Thin Man* films, based on the novel by Dashiell Hammett. Four of the *Thin Man* series' six films were helmed by Van Dyke.

Another cultural staple that owes its origins to *Manhattan Melodrama* is the song "Blue Moon." The melody appears in the picture, but is paired with different lyrics and is titled "The Bad in Every Man." After the film's release, famous songwriter Lorenz Hart was asked to change the lyrics so that they might be more pleasing to the general public; the song "Blue Moon" that we would recognize today was the result. **AKu**

► **Myrna Loy and Clark Gable, in this masterful combination of crime drama and romance.**

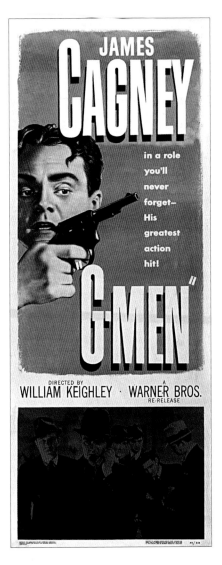

G-MEN 1935 (U.S.)

Director William Keighley **Producers** Louis F. Edelman, Hal B. Wallis, Jack L. Warner
Screenplay Seton I. Miller (based on Darryl F. Zanuck's novel *Public Enemy No. 1*)
Cinematographer Sol Polito **Music** Leo F. Forbstein **Cast** James Cagney, Margaret
Lindsay, Ann Dvorak, Robert Armstrong, Barton MacLane, Lloyd Nolan, William Harrigan

On July 22, 1934, federal agents killed the notorious bank robber John Dillinger outside the Biograph Theater in Chicago. Concerned about the rise of the celebrity criminal, of which Dillinger was a paradigm, in 1935 the Hays Office issued a moratorium on gangster films. *G-Men* was Hollywood's short-term solution for what to do with James Cagney. Worried about glorifying criminal violence? The solution is obvious: give the criminal a badge. Or, at least, give the actor who plays criminals a badge as an argument for why his real-life counterpart should be allowed to carry a gun. The strategy worked. The opening frames for *G-Men* proudly present its stamp of approval from the Production Code Administration. A mini-genre briefly flourished. The following year, *G-Men* director William Keighley sent another criminal-gone-G-man, Edward G. Robinson, undercover in *Bullets or Ballots* (1936).

Prefiguring the tension driving *The Departed*, in *G-Men* a gangster friend pays Brick Davis's (Cagney) way through law school with the proceeds of organized crime. Having achieved a law degree, but frustrated at a futile attempt to earn an honest buck as a lawyer, Cagney joins the FBI to help solve the

◄

Facing criticism of making heroes out of gangsters, Warner Bros. switched to the perspective of the law enforcer in this movie.

murder of a close pal. Brick's criminal benefactor goes straight and opens a rural lodge, much like the one in Wisconsin that the Dillinger gang used as a hideout. Nevertheless, Brick is tainted by the underworld figures of his childhood (and to some extent with Cagney's past roles, such as Tom Powers in *The Public Enemy* [1931]). Some of Brick's superiors at the FBI suspect that Brick is an underworld mole, but by the end of the

"THE GANGSTER IS BACK, RACING MADLY THROUGH ONE OF THE FASTEST MELODRAMAS EVER MADE." *NEW YORK SUN*

picture he's able to redeem himself through heroic action. Although Brick carries a law degree, he's no sissy child of privilege. No, he's tough, smart, and physically capable. This comes as a shock to the other G-men, but we knew it before the movie starts. Cagney goes from being a public enemy to a public defender overnight. The transformation is key to understanding the effectiveness of the movie and much of Hollywood before, during, and since.

Movie stars often bring their reputation with them, along with a host of associations carried over from previous roles. Sometimes this can be distracting, but with Cagney it's almost always a treat. Although *G-Men* can't stand on its own as a movie, it doesn't have to. It rests on the shoulders of a small man's giant reputation—or as *Variety* magazine put it: "Cagney joins the government and cleans up the gangsters." **AS**

► James Cagney's role reversal in *G-Men* exploited his previous fame and reputation as a bad guy.

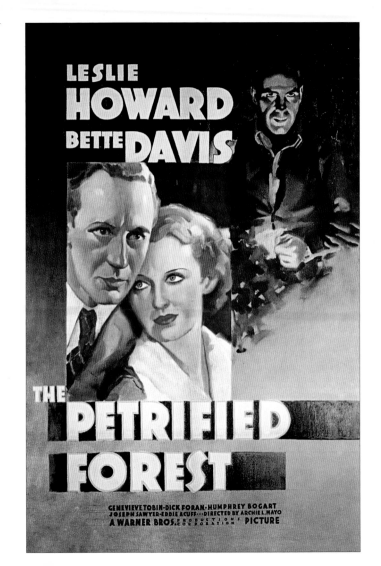

THE PETRIFIED FOREST 1936 (U.S.)

Director Archie Mayo **Producer** Henry Blanke, Hal Wallis **Screenplay** Charles Kenyon, Delmer Daves (from the play by Robert E. Sherwood) **Cinematography** Sol Polito **Music** Bernhard Kaun **Cast** Leslie Howard, Bette Davis, Humphrey Bogart, Genevieve Tobin, Dick Foran, Joe Sawyer, Porter Hall, Charley Grapewin, Paul Harvey

Now remembered chiefly for introducing Humphrey Bogart to the gangster movie, *Petrified Forest* is not really a gangster film as such, but rather an adaptation of a piece of serious American theater by Robert E. Sherwood, concerned more with ideas than action. The drama proper concerns the relationship between Alan Squier, a pessimistic English writer backpacking across America in search of existential enlightenment, and Gabrielle Maple, the pretty, talented, and intellectually stifled daughter of a way-station proprietor stuck in the heart of the American nowhere. The pair are played by Leslie Howard and Bette Davis, re-teamed after the previous year's *Of Human Bondage* ("Again they triumph!" screamed the publicity) and it is in the context of their story that the arrival of Bogart's snarling, scruffy Duke Mantee serves an almost symbolic function, as catalyst and liberator of repressed feelings and aspirations.

Both Howard and Bogart had played their roles on Broadway, but Warners' original intention had been to cast Howard only, opposite Edward G. Robinson. The star nobly made Bogart's casting a condition of his own, overriding considerable studio reluctance in an act of generosity that opened the door for

◀

Inspired by the theater, this movie introduced the poet idealist hero and the gangster antihero figures to Hollywood.

Bogart's subsequent starring career. (In gratitude, Bogart and Lauren Bacall named their first child Leslie.) With the action confined almost entirely to a single set and a few studio exteriors, the viewer is rarely likely to forget that this is essentially a piece of filmed theater. Dramatically, however, the resultant sense of claustrophobia does work somewhat to the film's advantage, and it is further notable for its surprisingly grim and

"THIS IS DUKE MANTEE, THE WORLD-FAMOUS KILLER—AND HE'S HUNGRY!" JACKIE

gloomy climax, along with its standardizing of the "gangster siege" plot that would turn up again in *Key Largo* (1948), *The Desperate Hours* (1955), and many others.

The cast is uniformly impressive, with Davis standing out in an uncharacteristically naïve and vulnerable role. But above all, it is Bogart's scene-stealing Mantee that leaves the strongest impression. In a performance somewhat different from later Bogart gangsters, the unshaven, ill-educated Mantee (apparently modeled on John Dillinger) has none of the actor's customary cynical cool; instead Bogart conveys a deep layer of insecurity, even regret, beneath a surface of thuggish bravado. In particular his relationship with Howard's character, which swings from indifference to contempt to confusion to grudging respect, is played with considerably more power and subtlety, by both actors, than may actually be present in the writing. **MC**

▶
Bette Davis and Leslie Howard comfort each other while held hostage by the gangsters. It was Howard who insisted that Humphrey Bogart be cast as Duke Mantee.

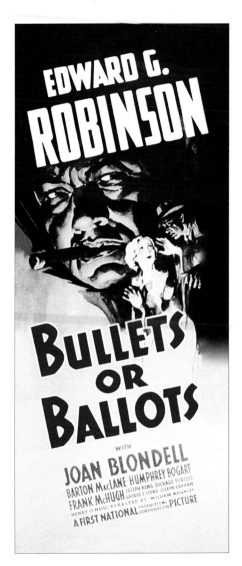

BULLETS OR BALLOTS U.S. (1936)

Director William Keighley **Producer** Louis F. Edelman **Screenplay** Seton I. Miller
Cinematography Hal Mohr **Music** M. K. Jerome, Bernhard Kaun, Heinz Roemheld
Cast Edward G. Robinson, Joan Blondell, Barton MacLane, Humphrey Bogart, Joe
King, Frank McHugh, George E. Stone, Louise Beavers, Richard Purcell, Joseph Crehan

This slick, pacy, complicated Warners programmer begins with
perhaps the studio's most impudent comment ever on the
relationship between screen and real violence, as crime baron
Barton MacLane and henchman Humphrey Bogart go to see a
"crime picture" together, actually a short in a fictional series
called "Syndicate of Crime," partially modeled on MGM's *Crime
Does Not Pay* films (1935–47), with Bogart commenting, "Wait till
you see the actor that takes you off."

It's a terrific opening to a film largely concerned with the
uneasy relationship between the media, the police, and
organized crime. The narrator of *Bullets or Ballots*, a crusading
publisher, is soon killed by Bogart's character because his
utilization of the film medium is proving too effective at
mobilizing public opposition to racketeering (one-nil to
Warners) and it's not long before we hear the police complaining
that the newly rendered transparency of their operations,
thanks to print media, is hampering their ability to deal with the
criminals. Accordingly, the plot is constantly advanced by
newspaper headlines, either referred to by the characters or
flying straight at the screen to the accompaniment of wailing

◀

**The poster makes
it quite clear who
the star attraction
was meant to
be in this vivid
gangster thriller.**

sirens and a background montage of cops racing to work. Since James Cagney had appeared to such memorable and popular effect in the previous year's *G-Men* (the obvious model for this film, also directed by Keighley and written by Miller), the latest Warner rouse was to recast their gangster icons as tough, no-nonsense good guys—that way they could maintain all the old attitudes, punchiness, and cocky dialogue (leaving the actual

"THE OLD CHIVALROUS SITUATIONS . . . ARE AGREEABLY TRANSLATED INTO SUB-MACHINE GUN TERMS." GRAHAM GREENE

criminality to the plainly irredeemable Bogart) and the censors couldn't complain. This one comes up with the even happier variation of casting Robinson as an undercover cop pretending to be a gangster (a deception the film does not even reveal until the halfway mark) so for whole sections it really *is* business as usual, perhaps the ultimate example of the studio having its cake and eating it too.

Warner Bros. were no doubt hoping for another *G-Men*-size hit, but lightning didn't manage to strike twice this time. Still, this remains an engrossing and hugely enjoyable yarn that rattles along at the best Warner Bros. tempo—all meat, no fat—with the help of a crackerjack studio supporting cast headed by Bogart in his first role after the same year's *Petrified Forest*, along with the great Joan Blondell, Frank McHugh, Louise Beavers, and the wonderfully greasy George E. Stone. **MC**

► **Ultimately, it was Bogart, playing the irredeemable gangster, who was on his way up the Hollywood tree.**

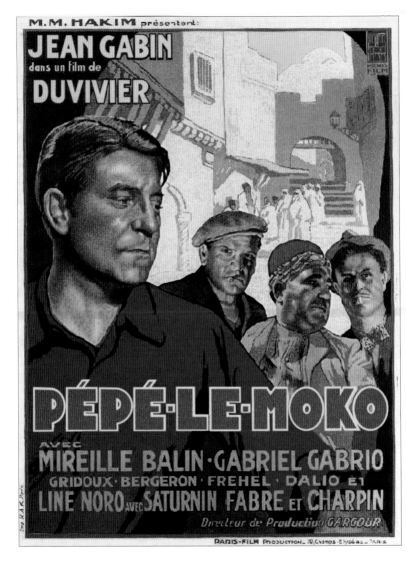

PÉPÉ LE MOKO 1937 (FRANCE)

Director Julien Duvivier **Producers** Robert Hakim, Raymond Hakim
Screenplay Henri La Barthe, Julien Duvivier, Jacques Constant
Cinematography Marc Fossard **Music** Vincent Scotto, Mohamed Ygerbuchen
Cast Jean Gabin, Mireille Balin, Line Noro, Lucas Gridoux, Gabriel Gabrio, Saturnin Fabre

With impressive "location" shooting (actually an impeccable set) and an iconic hero who is irresistible to the ladies, *Pépé le Moko* chronicles the final showdown with love and the law of a gangster who proves a doomed, proto *Pierrot le fou* (Jean-Luc Godard's 1965 crime drama). The seemingly endless maze of the casbah feels like a cage when everything you want suddenly stands outside it. Pépé (Gabin) operates according to the suave logic of the criminal playboy, which always serves him well—right up until it doesn't. After a recent spectacular heist, the authorities, particularly Inspector Slimane (Gridoux), are desperate to catch Pépé. Within Algiers' casbah he remains free, but once outside it he becomes vulnerable to the law. Scenes of working-class clamor on the hectic streets of Algiers and the gritty talk of Pépé's gang members add working-class allure to an otherwise glamorous portrayal of criminal life.

A lover of wealth and women, in that order, Pépé's mindset is best illustrated in the scene where he meets Gaby (Balin), the kept woman of an elderly curmudgeon. Enchanted, his eyes move from the jewels on her neck, ears, wrists, and fingers, to finally take in her lovely face. The ideal woman is a potential

◀

A world away from the Hollywood look, the poster reflects the French-colonial Algerian setting of the film.

victim, one who comes bedecked in luxury possibly for the taking. Pépé's real troubles begin with his desire for Gaby, who reminds him of Paris—that is, life outside the casbah. Though strictly faithful to no woman and no law, Pépé spends much of his time with Inès (Noro), a passionate, possessive Algerian woman whose embrace feels like house arrest once Pépé begins seeing Gaby. As Pépé pursues Gaby outside the casbah,

"OUR FRIEND SLIMANE IS FUNNY! HE MEANS IT! HE WANTS TO ARREST ME! DELUSIONS OF GRANDEUR." *PÉPÉ LE MOKO*

Slimane pursues Pépé, using the couple's assignations to ensnare him. There is more than a touch of xenophobic hatred in the Algerian, Muslim Slimane's pursuit of Pépé le Moko—Moko meaning "from Marseilles," that is, foreign.

Gabin as Pépé is the epitome of Gallic sexual aplomb. In one scene, flush with amorous feeling for Gaby, Pépé sings from his rooftop. The music resonates throughout the casbah, bringing smiles to the faces of the women, all of whom seem to be past conquests: when Pépé is happy, the casbah is happy. Unfortunately, this is a tragedy, not a musical, and in the end we are not sure if Pépé despairs more for the woman, or the life of crime that he must leave behind.

▶

Line Noro as Inès with Jean Gabin as Pépé. The movie was modeled on American gangster films, but has a poetic quality all its own.

An important film for cinema historians of "poetic realism" and often seen as a tranposition of the Hollywood gangster movie, *Pépé le Moko* is essentially a precursor of film noir. **HB**

MARKED WOMAN 1937 (U.S.)

Director Lloyd Bacon **Producers** Louis F. Edelman, Hal Wallis, Jack L. Warner
Screenplay Abem Finkel, Robert Rossen **Cinematography** George Barnes
Music Bernhard Kaun, Heinz Roemheld **Cast** Bette Davis, Humphrey Bogart,
Lola Lane, Isabel Jewell, Mayo Methot, Eduardo Ciannelli, Rosalind Marquis

In 1936, Special Prosecutor Thomas E. Dewey put Sicilian
mobster Lucky Luciano behind bars on prostitution charges.
Inspired in part by the real-life Lucky Luciano trial, *Marked
Woman* is an interesting attempt to play the Warner Bros.'
gangster formula from a female perspective (the intention was
presumably intended more to siphon some of the women's
picture market than to strike any kind of blow for equal
representation). A vehicle for Bette Davis—back at Warners
after her much-publicized walkout in protest at the poor quality
of parts she had been offered, and here given a role that mirrors
something of her actual feistiness and determination—the film
resembles a sub-plot from a standard Warners movie given
separate and independent life.

Davis plays a clip-joint hostess, the kind of character usually
seen on the periphery of the Warners universe, perhaps given
one good scene but nothing more, who refuses to testify at the
murder trial of her gangster boss, thus ensuring his acquittal.
But when her own sister is killed, she changes her mind and, in
a still-shocking development, is beaten and disfigured. The
switch of focus gives *Marked Woman* a refreshingly different

◄

**Rather than an
early feminist
victory, Bette
Davis' lead role
was more to do
with attracting the
female audience.**

feel, and provides several good roles for the studio's female contract artists (including Mayo Methot, soon to embark on her tempestuous marriage to Bogart). The prioritizing of Davis' character has an interesting side effect on the secondary casting as well. In the normal scheme of things, the crusading D.A. would have been lead material for Cagney or Robinson, but the role's secondary status means that it is taken by Bogart,

"I'LL GET YOU, EVEN IF I HAVE TO CRAWL BACK FROM THE GRAVE TO DO IT!" MARY DWIGHT STRAUBER

who thus gets to play his first upstanding character in a Warners crime movie. This then means that a star further still down the studio's roster of importance gets the traditional Bogart role of the vicious gangster (Ciannelli). With an all-star bill this would have been quite something; as it is, Ciannelli is rather colorless and Bogart can do little with his underwritten role, so Davis is left to carry the whole show.

Typically, Davis insisted on consulting doctors to ensure that her injuries looked authentic in the final scenes. Producer Hal Wallis was shocked by the result, complaining in a memo to Jack Warner that "[Seeing Bette Davis] with bandages on and her eyes made up is absolutely horrible... Let's stop trying to make her too horrible-looking." But Davis had her way as usual, and for most audiences her shocking appearance in the hospital is the most memorable thing in the picture. **MC**

► Bette Davis dominates Humphrey Bogart with a look, watched by Mayo Methot.

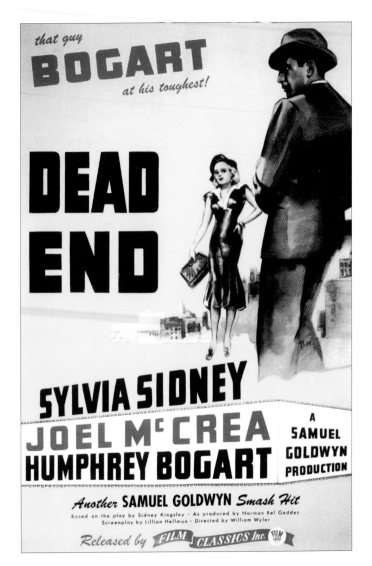

DEAD END 1937 (U.S.)

Director William Wyler **Producer** Samuel Goldwyn **Screenplay** Lillian Hellman (from the play by Sidney Kingsley) **Cinematography** Gregg Toland **Music** Alfred Newman **Cast** Sylvia Sidney, Joel McCrea, Humphrey Bogart, Wendy Barrie, Claire Trevor, Allen Jenkins, Marjorie Main, Billy Halop, Huntz Hall, The Dead End Kids

Audiences coming to this film on the strength of its advertising expecting another typical Bogart gangster movie may be disappointed to discover that it is in fact a social drama that just happens to have a Bogart gangster as one of the characters, and a secondary one at that. But they shouldn't, because it's an effective, sometimes moving and unusually serious piece of work, with an overt social conscience rare for a Hollywood movie of its time.

Adapted from a hugely successful play by Sidney Kingsley, *Dead End* is striking in its effort to convey, more vividly than any film made since the introduction of the Hays Code, a realistic portrayal of New York slum life: a world of poverty, casual violence, prostitution, and squalor, cleverly staged on stylized but brilliantly designed and photographed sets.

The film also addresses class tensions in an unusually frank manner, with Sylvia Sidney's Drina striking for better working conditions, and Joel McCrea's Dave, the former slum boy who trained as an architect and wants to build a new future away from the ghetto, torn between his feelings for Drina and his infatuation with Kay (Barrie), one of New York's upper set whose

◄

"Bogart at his toughest," announces the poster—although actually, it's more like life at its toughest, on the streets of New York.

town house overlooks the seedy tenements. Into this carefully delineated world comes Humphrey Bogart's "Baby Face" Martin, a notorious gangster on the run, returning home to flaunt his newfound affluence and catch up with his mother and old girlfriend Francey (Trevor). These scenes are among the most powerful in the entire film, and feature some of Bogart's best-ever acting work, as he is first tearfully rejected

"'ENEMIES OF SOCIETY' IT SAYS IN THE PAPERS. WHY NOT? WHAT'VE THEY GOT TO BE SO FRIENDLY ABOUT?" *CONNELL*

by his mother (Main)—who is now old, dejected, and repulsed by the man her son has become—and then horrified to discover that his old flame Francey has become a tired and wasted prostitute.

The film is also important for introducing the Dead End Kids, an ensemble of naturalistic teenage actors who would go on to take supporting roles in several Warner Bros.' future crime movies (notably *Angels with Dirty Faces* [1938]) and, ultimately—albeit in variously renamed and arranged conglomerations—in a series of increasingly comic second-feature vehicles of their own. First seen here, simply as the street gang that is exactly like the one in which both Dave and Baby Face started out, they represent the perpetuation of the crime and violence that the slums breed; a visual symbol of hopelessness and despair, for all their amusing banter and seeming lust for life. **MC**

► **Joel McCrea, Humphrey Bogart, and Allen Jenkins in this theatrical film set within 24 hours of New York's East Side life.**

ANGELS WITH DIRTY FACES 1938 (U.S.)

Director Michael Curtiz **Producer** Samuel Bischoff **Screenplay** John Wexley, Warren Duff (from a story by Rowland Brown) **Cinematography** Sol Polito **Music** Max Steiner **Cast** James Cagney, Pat O'Brien, Ann Sheridan, Humphrey Bogart, George Bancroft, Edward Pawley, Bobby Jordan, The Dead End Kids

Here we have the Warner Bros. crime movie formula in perfect working order. *Angels with Dirty Faces* features James Cagney and Pat O'Brien as former boyhood friends and small-time partners-in-crime Rocky Sullivan and Jerry Connolly, whose lives take very different paths when Rocky is sent to reform school. Rocky learns the tricks of the criminal trade while Jerry goes straight and becomes a priest.

Aware that their films were frequently condemned for glamorizing criminality in the eyes of youthful audiences, Warners here make this problem the central component of the narrative itself, as the friendship still retained by the two former pals is tested when Rocky's celebrity gangster becomes a hero to the gang of boys Jerry is trying to keep on the right side of the law. (Cast as the boys are the Dead End Kids in perhaps their most famous appearance outside of the original *Dead End* in 1937, noticeably less reprehensible after their debut appearance was itself widely criticized for providing bad role models.)

Much of the fun of these films is to be found in their attempts at providing authentic gangster thrills (provided in part here by Humphrey Bogart in one of his best pre-*Casablanca* sneering

◄

Combining gangster action and social conscience this movie is above all a shrewd and slick entertainment package.

hood roles) while at the same time maintaining an explicitly condemnatory attitude toward them to appease the censors, often taking the form of introductory scrolling captions claiming public service status. But the trick was rarely mastered as brilliantly as it was in this film, not least in its still almost unbearably powerful and moving final scenes. At the end of the movie, Rocky, sentenced to execution, aggressively refuses

"MORNING, GENTLEMEN. NICE DAY FOR A MURDER!"

ROCKY SULLIVAN

Jerry's pleas that he should pretend to be cowardly at the point of death, so the boys do not idolize and imitate him. With commendable ambiguity, we never discover for sure if Rocky really does turn yellow at the last minute or if his attitude of cocky bravado beforehand is all part of a performance to lend verisimilitude to his subsequent collapse. Most viewers, I suspect, lean toward the latter, more heroic option, but either way it is a shattering, audience-silencing climax to a film that never puts a foot wrong.

The Angels Wash Their Faces (1939) was a semi-sequel without the original male leads (it starred Ronald Reagan, who was a far less compelling substitute), but it retained Sheridan and the Dead End Kid who reform at the end, thus beginning the process of emasculation that would eventually turn them into comedy characters in their own series of second-feature vehicles. **MC**

► **Warner Bros. specialized in using cheap sets and shadows to great effect as seen here with James Cagney.**

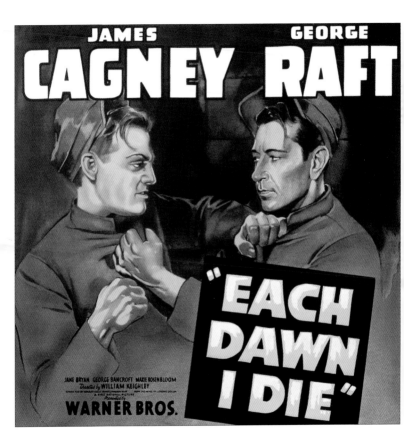

EACH DAWN I DIE 1939 (U.S.)

Director William Keighley **Producer** Hal B. Wallis **Screenplay** Norman Reilly Raine, Warren Duff, Charles Perry (based on the novel by Jerome Odlum) **Cinematography** Arthur Edeson **Music** Max Steiner **Cast** James Cagney, George Raft, Jane Bryan, George Bancroft, Max Rosenbloom, Stanley Ridges, Alan Baxter

James Cagney plays one of the good guys this time. Muckraking reporter Frank Ross (Cagney) gets an unwelcome chance to not only reveal but also experience real corruption when he is framed for drunken–driving homicide by a grafting district attorney whom Ross threatens to expose. Thrown into prison, Ross sees firsthand not just the violence and dishonesty with which the system treats its "victims," but also the cunning network of debts and vendettas that operates among his fellow prison inmates.

After being saved by Ross from ambush by a fellow prisoner, gangster "Hood" Stacey (Raft), in for a life sentence or two, remains protective of Ross. Despite an often vivid supporting cast, the chemistry between Cagney and Raft is unmistakable and the movie often seems a two-hander, charting the loyalties and betrayals between their characters as Hood plans his escape and Ross lobbies for vindication. Keighley makes effective use of the twine-making room where the prisoners labor, its nooks and crannies and the cover of official work allowing the prisoners to carry out many of their intrigues, and also providing the staging ground for the riot that ends the

◀
A two-star vehicle, this movie harks back to the Warner Bros. gangster heyday of the mid–1930s, before WWII changed how films looked forever.

movie. There is also a classic escape scene in a courtroom, ingeniously using a jump from a window, that pivots on Ross' inconveniently adamant careerism—he'll do anything for a good story—and Hood's ruthless will to survive.

But needling the viewer all the while is Cagney on the right side of the law. Sure, there's Cagney in *Yankee Doodle Dandy* (1942), but the Cagney we remember most is Cody Jarrett

"INJUSTICE IS RELATIVELY EASY TO BEAR; WHAT STINGS IS JUSTICE."

H. L. MENCKEN

mewling with grief and hatred after finding out about the death of his Ma, or, of course, Cagney as Tom Powers smashing a grapefruit in Kitty's face. Director William Keighley cleverly uses this tension to explore the film's themes: the fine line between justice and criminality, the turning point at which a righteous man might give up, having had enough. As the picture progresses, so does Ross' descent into the criminal mind. It is only when Ross is thrown in the dreaded hole — solitary confinement—that Cagney comes alive, positively vibrating with fury and indignation upon being let out once again into the light. Corruption comes from all sides.

In an interestingly bleak conclusion to the movie, Cagney—already disillusioned about justice—also loses his faith in friendship (thinking himself betrayed by Raft) and ends up going around the bend in solitary confinement. **HB**

► Cagney's role as Frank Ross takes him from keen reporter to humble prisoner and finally to a lonely, bitter, angry man.

THE ROARING TWENTIES 1939 (U.S.)

Director Raoul Walsh **Producers** Samuel Bischoff, Hal B. Wallis **Screenplay** Jerry Wald, Richard Macaulay, Robert Rossen **Cinematography** Ernest Haller **Music** Ray Heindorf, Heinz Roemheld **Cast** James Cagney, Priscilla Lane, Humphrey Bogart, Gladys George, Paul Kelly, Frank McHugh, Jeffrey Lynn, Elizabeth Risdon, Ed Keane

"When the legend becomes fact," said John Ford (in *The Man Who Shot Liberty Valance* [1962]), "print the legend." And what we have here is history being written by those who were there for the real thing and are now engaged in assigning it legendary dimensions. It is the final, irrevocable marriage of the real experience of the twenties, in all its facets and contradictions, and its mythic enshrinement by Warner Bros. over a decade of movies that defined the whole shape and rhythm of American crime cinema. Unlike its forebears, it presents itself not as a social issues picture, torn from the headlines, but as a nostalgic summation, complete with opening narration predicting that soon "people will say it never could have happened at all."

The Roaring Twenties is structured in three acts in the classic Warners manner, each linking the fate of the main characters to a wider historical moment. Act One deals with the First World War, and how it disrupts and changes forever the life paths of the main characters. Act Two brings us to Prohibition, by which James Cagney's Eddie Bartlett, returning home to an otherwise hopeless future, is able to use his vitality and ruthlessness to rise to a position of authority and affluence in the underworld.

◀

Athough the poster is classic 1930s, the subject is a decade younger. Among the last of the 1930s gangster cycle, stars and studio were in top form for this movie.

Finally, Act Three parallels his inevitable fall with the onset of the Great Depression, as he and the Roaring Twenties die together. Notable for its frantic pace and sense that in times of depression almost anyone is corruptible, *The Roaring Twenties* is a commentary on a decade of upheaval, sadness, and waste.

Cagney and Bogart may have had better roles individually, but they never sparked off each other more excitingly or

"I CAN JUST PICTURE YOU LIVING IN THE SUBURBS, WORKING IN A GARDEN . . . WOULDN'T THAT BE A LAUGH." PANAMA SMITH

assuredly as they do here. Cagney is the lead, as in all their joint ventures, giving Bogart a late chance to relinquish the elements of urban cool, which were already on the way to making a romantic lead of him, and wallow again in unabashed duplicity, sadism, and cowardice.

Bartlett, played with Cagney's usual, unique mix of arrogance and sympathy, is charming, at times almost vulnerable, and there is a constant sense that he would have happily lent his talents to some legitimate enterprise if only he could have found one, which lends his downfall a truly tragic grandeur. The final scenes, as he dies in the arms of Gladys George on a snowy flight of steps, have rightly joined those of Edward G. Robinson in *Little Caesar* (1931), Paul Muni in *Scarface* (1932), and Cagney himself in *The Public Enemy* (1931) as being one of the genre's most iconic last-act demises. **MC**

► Cagney (center) in control with McHugh (left) and Bogart (right) guarding their bootleg whisky.

HIGH SIERRA 1941 (U.S.)

Director Raoul Walsh **Producers** Mark Hellinger, Hal B. Wallis **Screenplay** John Huston, W. R. Burnett **Cinematography** Tony Gaudio **Music** Adolph Deutsch
Cast Ida Lupino, Humphrey Bogart, Alan Curtis, Arthur Kennedy, Joan Leslie, Henry Hull, Henry Travers, Jerome Cowan, Minna Gombell, Barton MacLane, Cornel Wilde

Co-written by W. R. Burnett, who had penned the original novel upon which Warners' breakthrough 1931 hit *Little Caesar* was based, and John Huston, the screenwriter and soon-to-be director who would start film noir in 1941 with *The Maltese Falcon*, *High Sierra* stands as a landmark of the gangster cycle by convincingly giving the sense of the end of an era.

As soon as Roy Earle, a notorious bank robber, is released from prison, he plots a new (and of course supposedly last) holdup at a smart Californian resort. Contrary to the classic gangsters of the previous decade, who first offered strong images of upward social mobility, Earle, played by a Humphrey Bogart going gray, is already on a downward path. He may be a living legend, but one who clearly belongs to the past. Whereas he used to hang around with Dillinger and the like, he is now forced to work with young, small-time crooks who lack self-control, and he receives orders from a dying (and soon dead) boss. *High Sierra* gave Bogart his first real star part (George Raft having originally turned it down). The movie also shows quite an interesting reversal of the usual female stereotypes. The apparently innocent, decent, and potentially redeeming young

◄
Both natural and human beauty conspire against ex-con gangster Roy Earle (Bogart) on his last job.

cripple Earle accidentally meets proves to be, in the end, a somewhat egocentric and debauched woman once she is cured. On the other hand, Marie (Lupino), the film's moll figure, who worked in a nightclub, will show compassion, fidelity, and love. Not without sentimentalism, Earle forms with Marie and a stray dog (who symbolically ends up in a cradle-like basket) a touching family of outcasts—the only family he can have.

"SUCH MEN ARE NOT GANGSTERS. . . THEY WERE A REVERSION TO THE WESTERN BANDIT." *W. R. BURNETT (WRITER)*

Like the Sterling Hayden character in Huston's *The Asphalt Jungle* (1950), Earle feels nostalgic for his father's farm, whereas the mobsters of the '30s were deeply rooted in an urban environment. However, this desire to find something closer to nature is ironically fulfilled. Hunted down like a wild animal, he ultimately takes refuge on Mount Whitney, where his journey will come to an end.

High Sierra looks back on the gangster by comparing him to a bandit of the American Old West. This anachronism is also hinted at later on in Joseph H. Lewis' *Gun Crazy* (1950), and is one that foreshadowed an entirely new wave of crime films. Earle's behavior expresses a need to get in touch with the world that surrounds him, a feeling of unease as well as a craving for something more—all characteristics that clearly anticipate film noir's themes of dislocation and deceit. **FL**

▶
"Babe" (Curtis), Roy Earle (Bogart), and "Red" (Kennedy) celebrate their heist.

THIS GUN FOR HIRE 1942 (U.S.)

Director Frank Tuttle **Producer** Richard Blumenthal **Screenplay** Albert Maltz, W. R. Burnett (from Graham Greene's novel *A Gun for Sale*) **Cinematography** John F. Seitz **Music** David Buttolph **Cast** Alan Ladd, Veronica Lake, Robert Preston, Laird Cregar, Tully Marshal, Mikhael Rasumny, Marc Lawrence, Olin Howlin, Roger Imhof

Alan Ladd and Veronica Lake were Paramount's Bogart and Bacall in a string of '40s noir thrillers, of which *This Gun for Hire* is the first and best. Ladd, Bogart's only serious rival as film noir's pre-eminent tainted hero until the arrival of Robert Mitchum later in the decade, has not been as well treated by posterity; he looks too delicate and baby-faced to be a tough guy, and at five-foot-five was even shorter than Bogart. Here, however, he cuts an impressively unsympathetic figure as Philip Raven, a hired killer whose aims correspond with those of the American government when he goes after a double-crossing client attempting to frame him for robbery—who also just happens to work for a gang of fifth columnists. En route, his path crosses with Lake's nightclub novelty chanteuse, acting undercover for the government and after the same man, whose policeman boyfriend is after Raven.

The Graham Greene story on which it is based has been Americanized and updated but with the author's cynicism and pessimism intact, perhaps therefore giving him certain paternity rights over what were soon to become the standard characterizations of film noir: devious, dangerous, and

◀

Despite fourth billing on this poster, it's Ladd's unsmiling contract killer and his relationship with Lake's undercover nightclub singer that's at the heart of the movie.

disappointed people in a shadowy world of seedy nightclubs, rainy streets, and Edward Hopper Automats, where hero status is strictly relative. The whole film has a bleakness that makes it a most unusual product of the war years—the villains may be enemy agents, but good guys are in conspicuously short supply. Ladd's Raven, though he does redeem himself to some extent, is a cold-blooded professional killer, pursuing the picture's main

"YOU'RE TRYING TO MAKE ME GO SOFT. WELL, YOU CAN SAVE IT. I DON'T GO SOFT FOR ANYBODY." *PHILIP RAVEN*

villain for reasons of purely personal revenge. We first see him at work in a chilling sequence in which he turns up at the apartment of his next hit to find the victim's innocent girlfriend unexpectedly present, and mechanically murders both.

The real hero is Lake's spunky Ellen Graham; by no means merely decorative, she is intelligent, brave, and resourceful (note how she creates a trail for the police to follow when Raven abducts her), and acting from selfless and honorable motives. She's also dazzlingly beautiful, and the only time the film stops frowning is during her fabulously eccentric nightclub numbers (dubbed by singer Martha Mears): "Now You See It, Now You Don't," performed while pulling cards, silk scarves, and canaries from nowhere and appearing and disappearing with trick photography, and "I've Got You," performed with a fishing rod, hat, and heart-stopping black PVC outfit. **MC**

► Adversaries or compatriots? Philip Raven (Ladd) manhandles nightclub singer Ellen Graham (Lake).

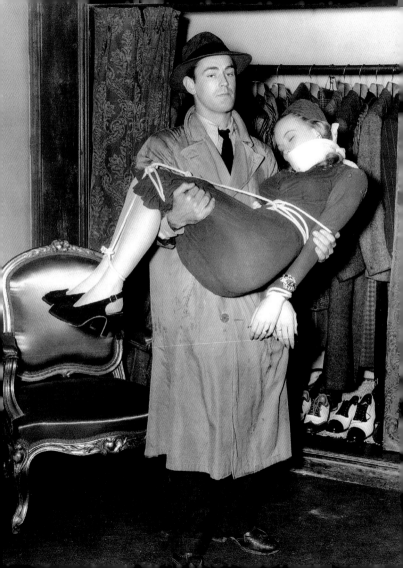

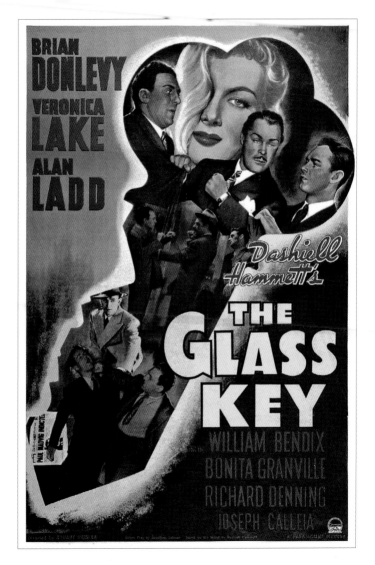

THE GLASS KEY 1942 (U.S.)

Director Stuart Heisler **Producers** Fred Kohlmar, Buddy G. DeSylva
Screenplay Jonathan Latimer (from the novel by Dashiell Hammett)
Cinematography Theodor Sparkuhl **Music** Victor Young, Walter Scharf
Cast Brian Donlevy, Alan Ladd, Veronica Lake, William Bendix, Richard Denning

In the wake of Warner Bros.' unprecedented success with John Huston's *The Maltese Falcon* (1941), Paramount Pictures, which during the 1930s had the reputation of producing the quintessential literary adaptations, quickly jumped on the "hard-boiled" bandwagon, securing the film rights to this relatively minor Dashiell Hammett novel.

Ed Beaumont (Ladd) is the strong arm to mobster Paul Madvig (Donlevy); during the Los Angeles municipal election, Madvig changes alliances from the relative conservative candidate to a firebrand reformer, Taylor Henry (Denning), specifically to get close to the candidate's beautiful daughter, Janet (Lake). When Janet's playboy brother, who is secretly dating Madvig's sister, turns up dead, Madvig is the prime suspect. Loyal to the end, Beaumont works overtime, including getting the stuffing knocked out of him by William Bendix in the film's most notorious scene, in order to clear his boss's name, and trying not to fall in love with Janet (as if that were possible). Looking and playing his usual deadpan, Ladd remains equally frozen, whether expressing his undying love for Lake or his loyalty to Donlevy. *The Glass Key* is not recognized

◄

This remake of Dashiell Hammet's novel, first filmed in 1935, paired Ladd and Lake in a tale of big–city political corruption.

as one of Hollywood's classic crime films, but it is fascinating to watch for the way it traces the emerging trends of the genre and as another vehicle for Alan Ladd's star status established in *This Gun for Hire* (1941). Although *The Maltese Falcon* certainly (and rightly) dominates the history, what we see from this minor work are the green shoots of film noir before it came to dominate Hollywood cinema by the mid-1940s, but without

"I JUST MET THE SWELLEST DAME . . . SHE SMACKED ME IN THE KISSER."

PAUL MADVIG

being distracted by the brilliance of Huston's film, or by Bogart's performance. Like *Falcon*, *The Glass Key* is shot mostly high-key—the dark, chiaroscuro lighting doesn't begin to dominate the genre for a few years yet; however the plot looks ahead to the classic period as an early version of the deadly noir love triangle. However, ever nervous about running afoul of the Production Code, Paramount decided to change the novel's ending to a much less cynical one, which is perhaps one of the reasons why the film isn't as well known as it otherwise might be.

On the flip side, if one tries to connect these early crime films not by cinema stylistics, but rather by theme, like Abraham Polonsky's later *Force of Evil* (1948), *The Glass Key* is an insightful document of mob involvement in local politics, a good thirty years before *The Godfather Part II* (1974). **MK**

► The lawless and the law: Ed Beaumont (Ladd) and D.A. Farr (MacBride).

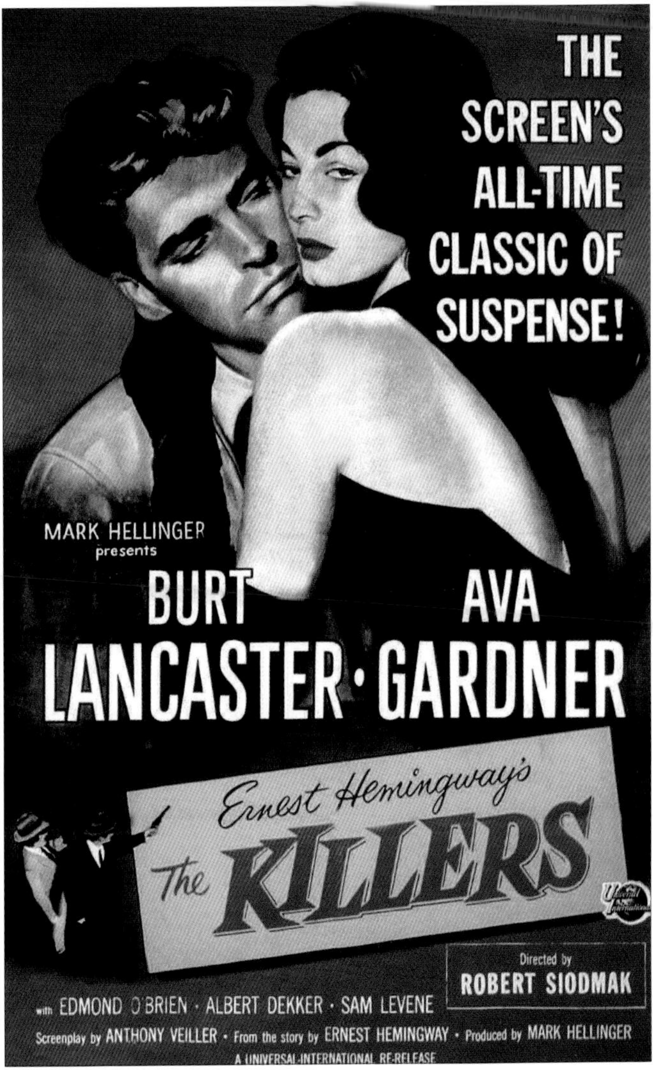
THE SCREEN'S ALL-TIME CLASSIC OF SUSPENSE!
MARK HELLINGER presents
BURT LANCASTER · AVA GARDNER
Ernest Hemingway's
The KILLERS
Directed by ROBERT SIODMAK
with EDMOND O'BRIEN · ALBERT DEKKER · SAM LEVENE
Screenplay by ANTHONY VEILLER · From the story by ERNEST HEMINGWAY · Produced by MARK HELLINGER
A UNIVERSAL-INTERNATIONAL RE-RELEASE

THE KILLERS 1946 (U.S.)

Director Robert Siodmak **Producer** Mark Hellinger **Screenplay** Anthony Vellier (from the short story by Ernest Hemingway) **Cinematography** Elwood Bredell **Music** Miklos Rozsa **Cast** Burt Lancaster, Ava Gardner, Edmond O' Brien, Albert Dekker, Sam Levene, Vince Barnett, Virginia Christine, Charles D. Brown, Jack Lambert

In *Planet Terror* (2007), Rapist #1 (Quentin Tarantino) tells Cherry Darling (Rose McGowan) that she looks like Ava Gardner. The reference is, in all probability, to Ava Gardner's Kitty Collins in *The Killers*; although the similarities between McGowan and Gardner are certainly not obvious, Darling does look like Collins in Siodmak's film.

Very loosely based on a 1920s short story by Ernest Hemingway, *The Killers* starts where Hemingway does, with two hired guns sitting in a roadside café looking for a man known as "The Swede" (Lancaster) whom they are to kill, while The Swede, aware of his fate, sweats out their inevitable arrival in his room. So ends Hemingway's story, with The Swede's death, but the movie is just getting rolling. Screenwriter Anthony Vellier (with uncredited contributions from John Huston) introduces an insurance adjuster, Jim Reardon (O'Brien), who is investigating The Swede's death. Something doesn't feel right to him, and so he digs a little deeper into the murder and by extension into The Swede's life as a promising boxer who finds himself sucked into the murky world of organized crime and femmes fatales.

◀

Announcing itself as "Ernest Hemingway's *The Killers*," the movie in fact extends the action way beyond the original short story on which it was based.

Like *Citizen Kane* (1941) before it, and *Memento* (2000) quite a bit after it, *The Killers* tells its convoluted story in reverse. As Reardon investigates The Swede's murder, he interviews an old childhood friend of the murdered man's, a Lt. Sam Lubinski (Levene), who tells him of a heist he was investigating that The Swede might have been involved in. This information leads Reardon to Big Jim Colfax (Dekker), a career criminal,

"DON'T ASK A DYING MAN TO LIE HIS SOUL INTO HELL."

LT. SAM LUBINSKY

and his moll Kitty Collins (Gardner). Like most classic noirs, the question of whose side Collins is on—Colfax's or The Swede's—depends on which way the wind is blowing. The Swede, believing that Collins really loved him, double-crossed Colfax out of his cut, which in turn is what motivated Colfax to call the "killers" to town.

It is hard to believe, sixty-plus years later, that *The Killers* was Lancaster's first picture; his star power is evident from the first dark and sweaty moments of the film. His performance is nuanced and quiet, while equally displaying a powerful anger that seems to bubble not far from the surface.

The Killers is a worthy production to be saddled with the frequently overused sobriquet "classic." Defining film noir in its dark and shadowy visual construction, it is also a prime example of post–World War II pessimism and fatalism. **MK**

► "Swede" Anderson (Lancaster) with Kitty Collins (Gardner) exposed to the classic film noir lighting of Elwood Bredell.

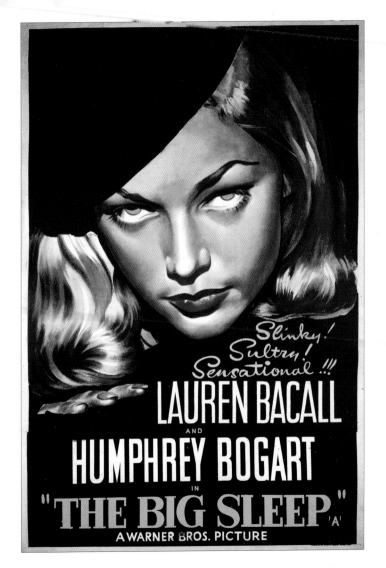

THE BIG SLEEP 1946 (U.S.)

Director Howard Hawks **Producer** Howard Hawks **Screenplay** William
Faulkner, Leigh Brackett, Jules Furthman (from the novel by Raymond Chandler)
Cinematography Sidney Hickox **Music** Max Steiner **Cast** Humphrey Bogart, Lauren
Bacall, John Ridgley, Martha Vickers, Dorothy Malone, Elisha Cook Jr., Charles Waldron

A treasure trove of great lines, iconic performances, gloriously
moody photography, and some of the most labyrinthine plot
developments ever foisted upon a Hollywood movie, *The Big
Sleep* has as strong a claim as any to the title of greatest crime
movie ever made.

You think first, obviously, of Bogart as Philip Marlowe:
sardonic, disillusioned, resourceful, cynical, yet possessed of a
kind of battered nobility. You think of Lauren Bacall, in the
second and most effective of their big-screen teamings, and
of their dialogue, impeccably delivered and bristling with
sexual innuendo. Then you recall the Warner noir universe, of
shadows and rain and fog, high collars and felt hats, small-
time crooks and girls on the make, where nobody can be
trusted and everybody lies all the time.

But this is one of those movies where virtually every line is
quotable, just as every scene is a separate delight and every
character gets their own chance to shine. Think of Dorothy
Malone's cameo as the bookstore salesgirl who passes a
boozy afternoon with Marlowe; of Elisha Cook Jr. as Jonesy,
the patsy whose efforts to get in on the action leave him

◄

As iconic as the
movie itself, the
poster oozes class
in its understated
execution.

dead, or of Martha Vickers as Carmen, Bacall's thumb-sucking, nymphomaniac younger sister. Then reflect on how Charles Waldron's General Sternwood, forced to live in an orchid house after a lifetime's dissipation and debauchery, is able to leave such an indelible impression despite appearing in only one scene; or that Sonia Darrin's touching Agnes, the girl who never gets the breaks, is not even listed in the credits.

"ALL [BOGART] HAS TO DO TO DOMINATE A SCENE IS TO ENTER IT."

RAYMOND CHANDLER

Though the story of Chandler confessing that even *he* didn't know who killed the chauffeur is surely apocryphal (it's not *that* hard to work out!), this is a dense and intricate plot for sure, made more so by the dictates of censorship. (You have to guess for yourself, for instance, that Carmen is both a drug addict and is embroiled in a pornography racket, a vitally relevant fact that the film merely implies opaquely.) Still, even if you don't follow every twist, it is unlikely you'll be feeling shortchanged come the breathtakingly tense final scene, notable for one of the most shockingly effective moments of implied violence in Hollywood history. The whole film is a lesson in how to achieve and sustain mood, style, and excitement without once violating the dictates of the Production Code or setting foot outside a studio soundstage. One of the greatest mainstream noir films ever made. **MC**

► **Bogart pieces together the clues in this film noir masterpiece.**

KISS OF DEATH 1947 (U.S.)

Director Henry Hathaway **Producer** Fred Kohlmar **Screenplay** Ben Hecht, Charles Lederer, Eleazar Lipsky (story) **Cinematography** Norbert Brodine **Music** Norbert Brodine **Cast** Victor Mature, Brian Donlevy, Coleen Gray, Richard Widmark, Taylor Holmes, Karl Malden, Anthony Ross, Dort Clark, Iris Mann, Howard Smith, Robert Adler

As the film begins, a woman's voice informs us that it is Christmas Eve, and that Nick Bianco (Mature) has not worked in a year and has a prison record. Nick, the voice says, has gone Christmas shopping for his kids; in other words, Nick is taking part in a jewelry heist. The getaway from the job goes awry, and Nick is shot and captured. The voice tells us that the same thing happened to Nick's father, and that young Nick saw it happen. Nick, it seems, is the product of a bad environment and cannot escape his criminal past.

Kiss of Death thus begins as a conventional exercise in Hollywood liberalism. Even Assistant District Attorney Louis D'Angelo (Donlevy) wants to help. Nick has two girls; D'Angelo cannot believe that the father of such children is a born crook. Crooked, yes, but not a crook. D'Angelo offers him a deal, but Nick refuses to squeal. Nick goes off to prison, handcuffed to Tommy Udo (Widmark). Yet we find that liberalism has its limits. No narrator's voice pleads on Udo's behalf, and no one offers him a deal. Udo is just an irredeemable crook. Nick's wife commits suicide because his criminal associates have not been taking care of his family. Nick now agrees to squeal to gain his

◀

The melodramatic poster art highlights the film's psychopathically sadistic aspects, represented by Tommy Udo (Widmark).

parole. Tommy Udo, no longer in prison, is sent to deal with the man mistakenly thought by the gang to be the squealer. The man has skipped town, but Udo, in what is still a shocking scene, gleefully pushes the man's wheelchair-bound mother down the stairs. Her murder, he figures, should put an end to the squealing for good. We then learn that Nettie Cavallo (Gray), once the babysitter for Nick's girls, is the film's narrator. She has

"I LET 'EM HAVE IT IN THE BELLY, SO THEY CAN ROLL AROUND FOR A LONG TIME THINKIN' IT OVER." TOMMY UDO

long loved Nick, and they get married after he is paroled. All goes well until Nick testifies against Udo. Udo is acquitted, and Nick knows that Udo will eventually find him or, even worse, Nettie and the girls. Nick goads Udo into shooting him in front of the police, who themselves shoot Udo. Udo will go to prison, and Nick will eventually return home.

Richard Widmark's screen debut as Tommy Udo makes *Kiss of Death* more than just a well-honed genre picture. Udo's giggling, sadistic love of violence dominates the movie. Consequently, we tend to forget that Victor Mature gave one of the best performances of his career, seeing how thoroughly he was upstaged by Widmark.

Another notable feature of this production was the way in which the movie impressively marked the transition from stagey studio painted sets to filming in real locations. **CB**

►
Shadows and light: Nettie Cavallo (Gray in her screen debut) and Nick Bianco (Mature).

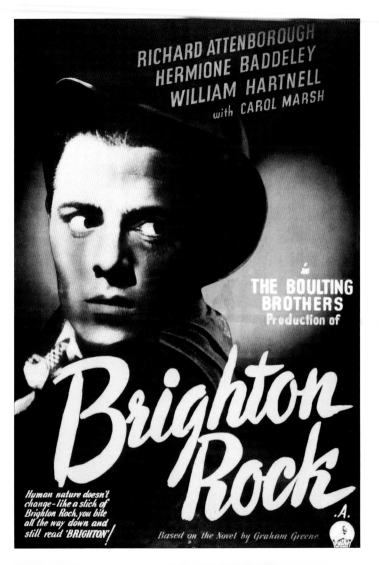

BRIGHTON ROCK 1947 (U.K.)

Director John Boulting **Producer** Roy Boulting **Screenplay** Graham Greene, Terence Rattigan (based on Graham Greene's novel) **Cinematography** Harry Waxman **Music** Hans May **Cast** Richard Attenborough, Hermione Baddeley, Harcourt Williams, William Hartnell, Carol Marsh, Nigel Stock, Wylie Watson

Graham Greene was always dismissive of the cinema as a "trivial" art form, and he wrote *Brighton Rock* to be, in many respects, his commentary on the kind of crime films coming over from Hollywood, which he had little time for. So what we have with *Brighton Rock*, the novel certainly, and to a greater extent, the film, is the British trying to outdo the Americans at the genre they invented.

The plot of *Brighton Rock* is fairly simple: a vicious hoodlum with the incongruous name of Pinkie (Attenborough) marries a sweet and innocent young girl, Rose (Marsh), so she cannot testify against him for a murder he committed at an amusement park. Pinkie's gang is quickly losing power and influence in this British seaside town to the increasing Italian (read Mafia, read even further *American*) presence within organized crime, and the possibility that Pinkie can no longer murder with relative impunity is evidence of that waning power. Added into the mix, a local showgirl, Ida (Baddeley), knows something fishy is going on and takes on the role of amateur detective to investigate this murder. *Brighton Rock*, although certainly a crime drama, is often more like a horror film because of its

◀

To avoid any possible problems with its very English title, the film was released in the U.S. as *Young Scarface*.

overall tone and atmosphere; in a sense, a kind of *Gothic* crime drama. Attenborough's portrayal of Pinkie is a terrifying depiction of a teenage sociopath, which never degenerates into maudlin social preaching so often the norm in films of this period. What makes Pinkie so frightening is his complete lack of a moral core. No attempt is made to explain the motivation for his violence; he is simply wired wrong. His recording of a "love

"IT PROCEEDS WITH THE EFFICIENCY, THE PRECISION, AND THE ANXIETY TO PLEASE OF A CIRCULAR SAW." *DILYS POWELL*

letter" to Rose into an instant phonograph machine is arguably one of British cinema's creepiest moments, and the film caused quite a stir at the time.

Although the film starts off with fairly typical British B movie banality in its cinematography, the occasional moments of quasi-expressionist excess become increasingly prevalent as the story progresses. There is more than a passing similarity between *Brighton Rock* and Fritz Lang's Weimar crime drama, *M* (1931); both films draw the audience into a criminal underworld depicted through canted camera angles, dark apartment corridors, and chiaroscuro lighting. Beautifully shot by Harry Waxman, it's perhaps the nearest thing to a British noir thriller and has the authentic tang of fish-and-chips. The murder sequence inside the "Dante's Inferno" ghost house ride is one of the best examples of British expressionist cinema. **MK**

► Richard Attenborough's portrayal of Pinkie is arguably his most memorable screen performance.

T-MEN 1947 (U.S.)

Director Anthony Mann **Producers** Aubrey Schenck, Turner Shelton
Screenplay John C. Higgins **Cinematography** John Alton **Music** Paul Sawtell
Cast Dennis O'Keefe, Mary Meade, Alfred Ryder, Wallace Ford, June Lockhart, Charles
McGraw, Jane Randolph, Art Smith, John Ardell, Vivian Austin, Louis Bacigalupi

T-Men can be considered a perfect example of the semi-
documentary pictures that were produced in the wake of the
success of *The House on 92nd Street* (1945), as well as an example
of the strong contradictions that informed some entries of this
subgenre. Before becoming a renowned western director,
Anthony Mann built his reputation in the '40s, thanks to a
convincing series of noir B movies. Made for Eagle-Lion Films,
T-Men tells the story of two Treasury Department agents who
have to go undercover in order to break up an important ring
that counterfeits both money and revenue stamps. The ensuing
meticulous investigation will lead them from Detroit to Los
Angeles and tragically will be resolved at high human cost.

The film's very beginning is a codified one that mobilizes
all the usual tricks—pompous music and voice-over, shots
of government buildings, a direct address to the spectator
by an official, the mention of the actual case on which the
film is based, etc. *T-Men* seems then to engage in a shameless
celebration of a government agency, a conformist stance
that is usually judged contrary to noir politics. However, as
soon as the investigation starts off, we enter a much darker

◄
**Said to be based
on several real–life
counterfeit scams,
this movie is the
best of Anthony
Mann's early work.**

world. One of the film's major assets is John Alton's black-and-white photography. For instance, Alton, who was working in perfect symbiosis with Mann, uses pronounced high and low angles, extreme close-ups, short focal lenses, images reflected in mirrors or windows, and unusual perspectives in order to create a disturbing environment that manages to subvert from within the inside the semi-

"THESE ARE THE SIX FINGERS OF THE TREASURY DEPARTMENT FIST. AND THAT FIST HITS FAIR, BUT HARD." ELMER LINCOLN IREY

documentary bias while still in a way remaining realistic. But *T-Men* is not only visually exciting. It offers a variety of precisely characterized villains (from bullies to a cold-blooded woman, and an invisible mastermind), but it also makes it clear that the undercover men are entrapped within their roles as mobsters (or are they at ease with them?). Dennis O'Keefe's agent appears as violent and sadistic as the nation's enemies. Far from the Hollywood canon, *T-Men* depicts acts of violence that are truly painful to see and that cannot be offset by few but intense moments of emotion.

► John Alton's characteristically unusual camera angles here framing Agent O'Brien (O'Keefe).

Finally, the film stresses the hierarchy that the agents discover inside the gang, and then points to a form of international gangsterism that takes on a deceitful veneer of respectability. After *T-Men*, both Mann and Alton would themselves move up to the apparently more respectable MGM productions. **FL**

I WALK ALONE 1948 (U.S.)

Director Byron Haskin **Producer** Hal B. Wallis **Screenplay** Charles Schnee
Cinematography Leo Tover **Music** Victor Young **Cast** Burt Lancaster, Lizabeth
Scott, Kirk Douglas, Wendell Corey, Kristine Miller, George Rigaud, Marc Lawrence,
Mike Mazurki, Mickey Knox, Roger Neury, Bobby Barber, John Bishop, Gino Corrado

After having spent fourteen years in prison, Frankie Madison
(Lancaster) comes back to New York and pays a visit to his old
partner in crime Noll Turner (Douglas) in order to get back his
share of the business they ran together. However, it doesn't
take very long before Frankie realizes that the rules of the game
radically changed while he was away.

As Martin Scorsese has aptly pointed out, the importance of
I Walk Alone in the gangster genre cannot be overemphasized.
Not only does it reveal the new "face" of gangsterism after the
war—a direction followed by a large number of later entries in
the genre—but it also openly discusses it through the telling
confrontation between its two male protagonists. Frankie is
the classic mobster from the Prohibition era, who is ready to
let the guns talk and believes in friendship and contracts
sealed by a simple handshake. While he was working with
Frankie, Noll sold smuggled rye whisky and beer, but his
activities are now out in the open. Noll, whose new
sophistication is epitomized by the fact that he speaks French
with his cook, has become a businessman with a veneer of
respectability. His smart nightclub enables him to hide his true

◀

This was the
first of many
movie pairings
of Lancaster and
Douglas. Unusually,
the billing in this
poster reflects their
respective roles;
later films billed
them more equally.

nature behind a string of complicated financial setups. Noll's relations with women also stress this transformation: instead of the sensual "torch singer'" who works in his club, he prefers to marry an older woman who belongs to high society and thus has connections. However, the opposition between the two characters leads to an ironic conclusion when a cunning Frankie uses Noll's own "weapons" to put him down.

"THE LOSS OF THE OLD-FASHIONED GANGSTER 'COMMUNITY' IS PART OF SUCH FILMS AS THIS." JONATHAN MUNBY

Based on a play by Theodore Reeves titled *Beggars Are Coming to Town* (with the screenplay written by Charles Schnee), this tale of betrayal and adjustment is a rather straightforward story that is mainly set inside Noll's Club. This choice (and the fact that the action takes place during a short period of time) could easily betray the material's origin, but it enables Haskin to visually translate the characters' confrontation onto the screen. For instance, he uses tight framing (with lamps in the forefront, etc.) to create a feeling of claustrophobia, and camera movements that seem to follow Lancaster and Douglas as if they were wild animals. Through the plate-glass window of Noll's office, we see a greenhouse full of plants that creep in a mist. This is probably the best visual metaphor for the city as human jungle found in the noir cycle, one that clearly hints at the reality hidden behind the new, faceless gangsterism. **FL**

► Burt Lancaster is given a beating by Wendell Corey.

DRUNKEN ANGEL 1948 (JAPAN)

Director Akira Kurosawa **Producer** Sojiro Motoki **Screenplay** Akira Kurosawa, Keinosuke Uegusa **Cinematography** Takeo Ito **Music** Fumio Hayasaka
Cast Takashi Shimura, Toshirô Mifune, Reisaburo Yamamoto, Michiyo Kogure, Chieko Nakakita, Noriko Sengoku, Shizuko Kasagi, Eitarô Shindô, Masao Shimizu

Although the cinematic style known as film noir is most frequently applied to a plethora of motion pictures that emerged in the United States during the 1930s, '40s, and '50s, it was by no means a phenomenon exclusive to Hollywood. In France, directors like Jules Duvivier (*Pépé le Moko* [1937]), Henri-Georges Clouzot (*Quai des Orfèvres* [1947]) and Jean-Pierre Melville (*Bob le Flambeur* [1956]) deployed noir motifs such as morally ambiguous characters, pessimistic narratives, and high-contrast black-and-white cinematography to astounding effect. Consequently, in the wake of its devastating loss in World War Two and dominated by U.S. cultural and political influence, some of the more compelling films to emerge from Japan were informed by noir sensibilities. Of these, Akira Kurosawa's *Drunken Angel* (a.k.a. *Yoidore Tenshi*) (1948) remains one of the most visually and thematically striking.

One of the first films over which Kurosawa was given significant creative control, as well as a work in which the legendary filmmaker "wanted to take a scalpel and dissect the yakuza," *Drunken Angel* tells the story of the tenuous relationship forged between Matsunaga (Mifune), a tubercular gangster

◄

Post-war Japan reinvented itself culturally with a hybrid of its warrior culture and Western gangsterism, epitomized in this early work of Akira Kurosawa.

looking to escape his violent lifestyle, and Doctor Sanada (Shimura), an alcoholic physician wary of the destructive warrior ethos he sees the yakuza as embodying. In keeping with many cinematic works classified as film noir, *Drunken Angel* avoids a simplistic good-versus-evil formula in favor of a plot grounded upon complex characters struggling to survive in a bleak urban environment, while battling personal prejudices and violent

"THE JAPANESE LOVE TO SACRIFICE THEMSELVES FOR STUPID THINGS."

DOCTOR SANADA

desires. These internal battles, and the external actions that mask or reveal them, are made all the more powerful as a result of the performance by the film's antiheroic leads, most notably Toshirô Mifune in his first collaboration with Kurosawa.

Despite its Western-influenced noir conceits, *Drunken Angel* is very much a film of its specific historical moment. Japanese audiences would recognize the occasional English-language signs, the prominence of Western clothing and the depiction of *pan pan* girls (prostitutes who specialized in servicing U.S. soldiers) as a subtle criticism of the U.S. influence. Similarly, in his depiction of Okada, the vicious and vengeful yakuza, spectators will discern an invective against a masculinist warrior ethos that, because of its influence upon Japan's imperialist pre-war legacy, contributed to the social and cultural chaos following Japan's surrender to Allied forces. **JM**

► The squalor of a broken nation provided the setting for this moving drama of sacrifice and redemption shot in an understated, realistic style.

KEY LARGO 1948 (U.S.)

Director John Huston **Producer** Jerry Wald **Screenplay** John Huston, Richard Brooks **Cinematography** Karl Freund **Music** Max Steiner **Cast** Humphrey Bogart, Edward G. Robinson, Lauren Bacall, Lionel Barrymore, Claire Trevor, Thomas Gomez, Marc Lawrence, Dan Seymour, Harry Lewis, John Rodney, Monte Blue, William Haade

Frank McCloud (Bogart) travels down to Key Largo in Florida to inform Frank Temple (Barrymore) of the circumstances surrounding the death in action of his son George, who had served under McCloud during the war. He finds the hotel Temple owns under the control of a group of gangsters led by Johnny Rocco (Robinson), who is dodging a deportation order. When the gangsters kill a local deputy, McCloud accepts to transport them to Cuba on his boat. Taking advantage of the situation on board, McCloud picks the gangsters off one by one and returns to Key Largo to marry George's widow (Bacall).

Key Largo is far less conventional a gangster movie than this summary suggests, and much of its interest lies in the way Huston and Brooks manage to exploit the codes of action, dress, and character to make a highly competent addition to the genre, while simultaneously endowing situations and dialogue with a dimension determined by the immediate post-war situation. This is achieved by a careful articulation of the twin themes of war and the struggle against fascism (of which George is the eloquent symbol) going back to the 1930s and the corrupting influence of gangsterism in both real life and the

◄

This movie transcends its single-scene theatrical origins with compelling performances from its star-laden cast.

cinema. It is crucial that Edward G. Robinson also played the title role in *Little Caesar* (1931). Although already important for the film's symbolic meaning that Rocco is outraged over being treated as an undesirable—"as if I was a Red"—the fact that two native Americans should be shot down as undesirables further compounds the film's bitter irony. Only the previous year Huston had founded with other Hollywood personalities the Committee

"ONE ROCCO MORE OR LESS ISN'T WORTH DYING FOR!"

FRANK MCCLOUD

for the First Amendment to combat the attempt by the House on Un-American Activities Committee to investigate communism in the film industry. *Key Largo* subtly shows the shift within Hollywood from an antifascist consensus toward one where new Cold War alliances excluded as hostile to corporate interests any commitment to the values that united Americans up to 1945.

Those in Hollywood who worked closely with gangsters throughout the 1930s to break unions and who felt that standing up for civil rights of such "undesirables" as Negroes and Indians was synonymous with communism, found themselves in charge again after the war, facilitating witch-hunting. The victory of McCloud is thus both wishful thinking on Huston's part and a tribute to a now lost commitment to those progressive values symbolized by George. **RH**

► Johnny Rocco (Robinson) relaxes in the tub, echoing his previous role in *Little Caesar*.

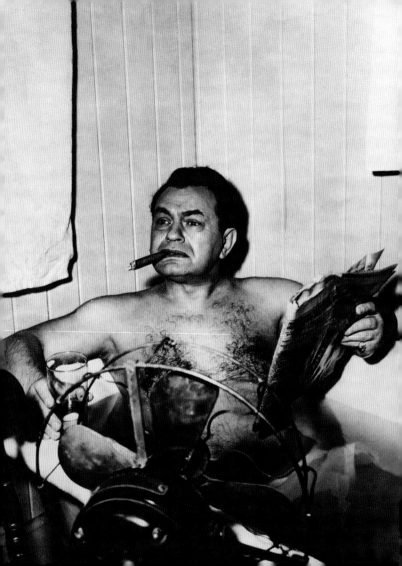

FORCE OF EVIL 1948 (U.S.)

Director Abraham Polonsky **Producer** Bob Roberts **Screenplay** Abraham Polonsky, Ira Wolfert **Cinematography** George Barnes **Music** David Raksin
Cast John Garfield, Beatrice Pearson, Thomas Gomez, Howland Chamberlain, Marie Windsor, Roy Roberts, Paul McVey, Tim Ryan, Sheldon Leonard, Stanley Prager

Before being brutally stopped by the government's anti-communist witchhunt in Hollywood, writer and director Abraham Polonsky's career had just taken a most promising turn with the now cult movie *Force of Evil*. In this rather short but dense film noir, John Garfield plays Joe Morse, a young lawyer who becomes too much mixed up in the shady business of one client. In order to finally fulfill the American Dream, Joe must make a legitimate corporation out of a much fragmented and low-yielding numbers racket, and somewhere along the way take care of his older brother Leo (Gomez).

Original and subversive as it is, *Force of Evil* nevertheless belongs to a group of post-war narratives that takes into account the evolution of organized crime into rackets that have the appearance of (or are dissimulated behind) a real business such as gambling. Joe's client, Ben Tucker (Roberts), is an old gangster from the Depression era (on several occasions, he is clearly associated with illegal beer smuggling, tommy guns, and bloody gangland murders) who is now trying to gain respectability and large sums of money through rationalization of costs and workforce. Joe himself is the one who is supposed

◄
A clinical analysis of the social, moral, and physical evils of the numbers racket, this movie is an attack on capitalism, depicted here by the racketeers.

to deal with the local authorities, as he offers an apparently unstained face. *Force of Evil*'s new form of gangsterism stands as a powerful metaphor of capitalism and America's forced centralization of institutions and enterprises since the war.

Central to the film is also a discourse about class differences. The upper-middle class of Joe and his partners is sustainably contrasted with the working class embodied by Leo. It confronts

"THE IDEA IS TO SHOW THAT IN AMERICA, CRIME IS PART OF THE BUSINESS." *ABRAHAM POLONSKY*

the dehumanizing way that people are often treated in corporations (everything from blackmailing to killing) with the warm caring that informs the relationship between the employees of the small bank run by the paternal figure of Leo— even the bookkeeper turned stool pigeon out of fear succeeds in arousing some kind of sympathy from the spectators. Although the dialogue, delivered by a strong cast that includes an always convincing Garfield, an emotionally profound Thomas Gomez, and an unusual Beatrice Pearson in the role of Joe's love interest, is sometimes particularly poetic, here Polonsky asserts himself above all as a strikingly visual director. For example, he makes fantastic use of sets and various New York locations in order to symbolically articulate on-screen the division between the two worlds he describes, as well as the ambitions of his cynical yet somewhat naïve protagonist. **FL**

► **Joe Morse was played by John Garfield, who is acknowledged as the predecessor of Method actors like Marlon Brando, James Dean, and Montgomery Clift.**

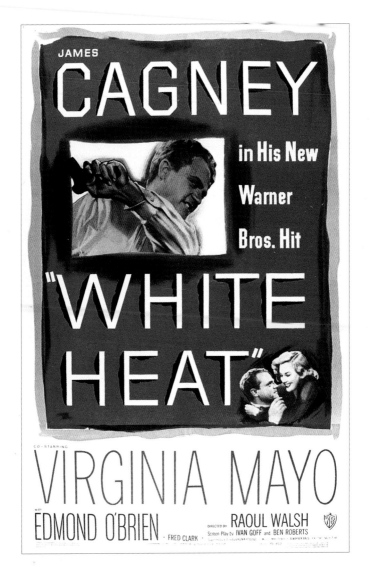

WHITE HEAT 1949 (U.S.)

Director Raoul Walsh **Producer** Louis F. Edelman **Screenplay** Ivan Goff,
Ben Roberts (from a story by Virginia Kellogg) **Cinematography** Sidney Hickox
Music Max Steiner **Cast** James Cagney, Virginia Mayo, Margaret Wycherly, Steve
Cochran, John Archer, Fred Clark, Edmond O'Brien, Wally Cassell, Marshall Bradford

The first of two starring vehicles (the other being the following
year's *Kiss Tomorrow Goodbye*) that marked James Cagney's
return to the gangster genre after a decade of diversification,
White Heat is a noticeably more brutal film than any of its kind
since the pre-Code originals, having inherited something of
the nihilism of post-war film noir. The 1930s gangster movie
sought constantly to justify itself against a prevailing climate of
moral censure; now, with censorship somewhat liberated after
the war, it was free to let rip again.

Played by an older, rounder Cagney with mesmerizing
energy and what can only be described as relish, Cody Jarrett is
a mother-fixated psychopath entirely devoid of redeeming
characteristics, given to sudden outbursts of sadistic violence
and frequent brainstorms that leave him clutching his head
and screaming in agony.

Jarrett is also sexually ambiguous to a degree far more
explicit than might be expected from a film of its time. He has
a wife, Verna (a bewitching, doll-like Virginia Mayo) but mainly,
we sense, for appearance's sake ("Ain't never been nobody but
Ma," he explains at one point). Although his relationship with

◀

White Heat
equals *Scarface*
plus *Psycho*. This
flammable formula
provides a fitting
conclusion to the
1930s gangster
genre, albeit nearly
a decade later.

his mother is far too weird to permit a straightforwardly sexual reading, there are clear hints of homosexuality in his attachment to Hank Fallon (O'Brien), a cop working undercover as a member of Jarrett's gang. Caught attempting to sneak out and warn the police of Jarrett's latest plan, Fallon excuses himself by claiming he is merely intending to visit his wife for a few hours. Jarrett believes him, but displays unmistakable signs of disappointment

"HE FINALLY GOT TO THE TOP OF THE WORLD—AND IT BLEW RIGHT UP IN HIS FACE." HANK FALLON

and jealousy before immediately taking Verna to bed, whereupon she emerges next day purring with contentment.

His mother (Wycherly) is more than merely complicit in his criminal activities—she is an active instigator of them, modeled on the real-life Ma Barker. The scene where she and Jarrett coldly decide to kill rather than leave behind a wounded gang member is especially chilling in the light of Hollywood's customary sentimental respect for the institution of motherhood.

A triumphant return to form for both Cagney and the Warner Bros. gangster movie, *White Heat* retains the power to stun audiences with its violence, tension, and the excellence of its lead performance. Memorable moments include Jarrett's one-man prison riot after hearing the news of his mother's death, and of course the explosive finale complete with now-legendary last words: "Made it, Ma—top of the world!" **MC**

▶
Going out in a blaze of glory: Arthur "Cody" Jarrett (Cagney).

THEY LIVE BY NIGHT 1949 (U.S.)

Director Nicholas Ray **Producer** John Houseman **Screenplay** Nicholas Ray, Charles Schnee (based on the novel *Thieves Like Us* by Edward Anderson) **Cinematography** George E. Diskant **Music** Leigh Harline, Woody Guthrie **Cast** Cathy O'Donnell, Farley Granger, Howard Da Silva, Jay C. Flippen, Helen Craig

This little-known film, Nicholas Ray's directorial debut, has been recognized as a sensitive romance and as an early film noir from RKO studios. The preoccupations of Ray's subsequent work are immediately identifiable in *They Live by Night*, which maps the fate of young social misfits in a corrupt society.

Lest there be any doubt, a prologue with shots of a young couple, lit by a flickering fire, announces that "this boy and this girl were never properly introduced to the world we know," and then the scene cuts to a "God" shot of a car filled with men, traveling on a road to nowhere. After a blowout, the injured young escaped convict, Bowie (Granger), hides out under a billboard and is rescued by the monosyllabic, suspicious Keechie (O'Donnell), her femininity disguised in men's overalls and a slouch hat. The attraction between Keechie and Bowie is evident, but the film is marked by the era's Production Code, so the couple's intimate moments are underscored by the theme of the Irish folk song "I Know Where I'm Going."

The couple share a history of inadequate fathers and treacherous mothers, but they are still depicted as unscarred innocents following an impossible dream; the "couple on the

◄

A passionate, lyrical, and imaginative film from the opening aerial shot tracing the escaped convicts' car to the inexorable climax.

run" theme becomes a question of destinations rather than escape. The two more cynical older convicts have "invested" in Bowie, knowing that a bank robbery is a three-man trick. Bowie dreams of a lawyer who will clear him of his murder charge, a fantasy annulled by inaccurate media coverage, to be replaced by the mirage of Mexico. The young couple are on the run, and despite Keechie, Bowie is unable to extricate himself from his

> ## "IN A WAY I'M A THIEF JUST THE SAME AS YOU ARE, BUT I WON'T SELL YOU HOPE WHEN THERE AIN'T ANY." MR. HAWKINS

fellow gangsters, driven by his own moral code. We are constantly reminded that they are all "thieves like us." Keechie's pregnancy is debated in a veiled reference to knitting needles and Bowie's naïve comments regarding her weight gain, and is "normalized" by a cut-rate wedding undertaken on the spur of the moment. In a suggestive shot the couple crosses the road from a fast-food restaurant to the wedding parlor. The suspicious pastor asks about their destination, and Keechie firmly declares, "We know where we're going."

Ultimately, *They Live by Night* displays the conflict of two opposing codes of loyalty. Bowie, as the naïve gangster outsider, ultimately cannot be reincorporated into a society that in any case is typically composed of "thieves like us." And because the devotion of the good woman goes unrewarded, the film's tragic ending is inevitable. **VC**

▶
Cathy O'Donnell and Farley Granger are on the run, heading for tragedy.

GUN CRAZY 1950 (U.S.)

Director Joseph H. Lewis **Producers** Frank King, Maurice King **Screenplay** MacKinlay Kantor, Dalton Trumbo **Cinematography** Russell Harlan **Music** Victor Young **Cast** John Dall, Peggy Cummins, Harry Lewis, Nedrick Young, Anabel Shaw, Berry Kroeger, Morris Carnovsky, Russ Tamblyn, Trevor Bardette, David Bair, Tony Barr

Bart Tare (Dall) has been obsessed with guns all his life, but not with killing. The impulsive theft of a revolver lands him in reform school for four years, and then he goes into the army. After Bart gets out of the service, he goes to a carnival with his childhood friends Clyde Boston (Lewis) and Dave Allister (Young). There he meets Annie Laurie Starr (Cummins) and bests her in an onstage shooting competition. Their instant mutual attraction quickly turns to obsession.

Bart and Annie Laurie are obviously a match made in hell. They get married, but when their financial luck runs out, Laurie declares that she will leave him unless he agrees to a life of crime with her. She says that she wants to do a little living, but what she really wants is action. Because Bart cannot bear to lose her, he reluctantly goes along. They begin with simple stickups and then graduate to doing more elaborate robberies. The violence escalates until Annie Laurie kills two people during the couple's last heist.

The pair know that it would be safer to split up, but their obsession is so intense that they cannot bear to be apart. As Bart puts it, they go together like guns and ammunition. When

◄

A.k.a. *Deadly Is The Female*, the movie is loosely based on Bonnie and Clyde. Without star names, the poster had to exploit provocative imagery and strident graphics.

they are unable to cross into Mexico, they seek refuge with Bart's sister Ruby (Shaw). Clyde and Dave go to Ruby's on a hunch, forcing Bart and Annie Laurie to flee. They ultimately find themselves trapped in a swamp, surrounded by the police. Dave and Clyde try to persuade them to give up. When Annie Laurie is about to shoot the two men, Bart shoots her dead in order to save his friends. He is then killed in a hail of bullets.

"WE GO TOGETHER, ANNIE. I DON'T KNOW WHY. MAYBE LIKE GUNS AND AMMUNITION GO TOGETHER." *BART*

Working on a tight budget, Joseph Lewis directed *Gun Crazy* with imagination and skill, without recourse to large set pieces and hordes of extras. In a famous scene, Bart and Annie Laurie drive into town, rob a bank, and then speed away. Shot in a single take lasting three-and-a-half minutes, the camera stays in the backseat of their car the entire time. The robbery of a meat-packing plant and the final scene in the swamp are equally compelling sequences.

Gun Crazy is utterly frank about the connection between sex and violence. Unlike most couples on the run, Bart and Annie Laurie thrive on their dangerous life, even though, of course, they also want to escape it. But we know that they will eventually die hard and bloody. After all, no other end could really satisfy them. Intense and subversive, *Gun Crazy* is more gripping than its progeny, *Bonnie and Clyde* (1967). **CB**

► **Much of the film's energy springs from the chemistry and improvised dialogue in some scenes between Peggy Cummins and John Dall.**

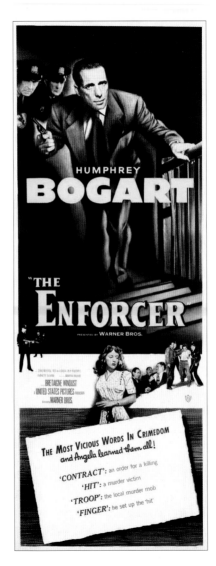

THE ENFORCER 1951 (U.S.)

Director Bretaigne Windust (and Raoul Walsh, uncredited) **Producer** Milton Sperling
Screenplay Martin Rackin **Cinematography** Robert Burks **Music** David Buttolph
Cast Humphrey Bogart, Zero Mostel, Ted de Corsia, Everett Sloane, Roy Roberts,
King Donovan, Michael Tolan, Bob Steele, Adelaide Klein, Don Beddoe, John Kellogg

In *The Enforcer*, Humphrey Bogart stars as Martin Ferguson, an
assistant district attorney on the verge of breaking a big case
thanks to a single key witness named Rico (de Corsia). However,
this henchman soon falls to his death while, out of terror, he
tries to escape. Given that it's only a few hours until the trial,
Ferguson decides to spend the night looking in his files for a
possible overlooked clue.

Directed by Bretaigne Windust, although Raoul Walsh
stepped in when he fell ill (or, according to others, was fired),
The Enforcer stands as a good example of the Warner Bros.
"social problem" film. Things had changed since the early 1930s
and the release of the classic gangster films (such as *Little
Caesar* and company): in 1950 the Senate Special Committee
to Investigate Crime in Interstate Commerce, headed by Estes
Kefauver, began hearings that revealed the existence of
organized crime to Americans—conspiracies being of course
highly topical during the McCarthy era and after the famous
Murder, Inc. trials. Much less romantic, and tragic, this form of
gangsterism is first hinted at in *The Enforcer* through a new set
of words ("hit," "contract") that are now known by every

◄

**Bogart's last
movie for Warner
Bros.—the studio
that made him a
star—is a well-
characterized story
based on fact.**

spectator but then puzzled the police officers. Central to this highly compartmentalized, nationwide phenomenon was anonymity, whereas previous gangs relied heavily upon their charismatic leaders. *The Enforcer* offers a complete manual that gives the impression of revealing on–screen every cog in this new corporation, notably through the eyes of outsiders—Ferguson and his colleagues.

> ## "SOMETIMES I MEET A GUY AND THEN I NEVER SEE HIM AGAIN. I GOT A BIG TURNOVER IN FRIENDS." *RICO*

Despite an extreme educational bias, being shot by Robert Burks in a semi-documentary style, and featuring a laconically witty script by Martin Rackin, *The Enforcer* also manages to be a tense thriller. From this latter standpoint, the beautifully shot first fifteen minutes, where Rico is terrified by the surrounding tribunal, are exemplary, with Raoul Walsh restaging the climactic shootout. It successfully manages to convey the pervasive terror and paranoia that the organization inspired by the Murder, Inc. case created. As Rico puts it, Albert Mendoza (Sloane), the business inventor, "ain't human" (and his name isn't Anglo-Saxon), which is an obvious way of separating him from the rest of society—other members are all humans because in the end they can feel fear. How can one take down such a monster? As is often the case in crime films, although for quite different reasons here, *cherchez la femme*. . . . **FL**

► D.A. Martin Ferguson (Bogart) administers justice on Joseph Rico (De Corsia).

THE LAVENDER HILL MOB 1951 (U.K.)

Director Charles Crichton **Producer** Michael Balcon **Screenplay** T. E. B. Clarke **Cinematography** Douglas Slocombe **Music** Georges Auric **Cast** Alec Guinness, Stanley Holloway, Sid James, Alfie Bass, Marjorie Fielding, Edie Martin, John Salew, Ronald Adam, Arthur Hambling, Gibb McLaughlin, John Gregson, Clive Morton

The Lavender Hill Mob is one of the best-loved Ealing films, and along with *The Man in the White Suit*, which also starred Alec Guinness, it marked 1951 as a peak year for the studio. The impeccably crafted, Oscar-winning screenplay was a high point for T. E. B. Clarke, who also wrote *Passport to Pimlico* (1949), *Hue and Cry* (1947), and *The Titfield Thunderbolt* (1953) for Ealing.

The film's main protagonist is Henry Holland (Guinness), a City of London bank clerk who has for twenty years been responsible for supervising gold bullion deliveries. Yearning to be a millionaire but having to be "satisfied with eight pounds, fifteen shillings, less deductions," Holland has cultivated a reputation as a trustworthy if unambitious custodian while honing a plan to rob the bullion van. However, his plan is incomplete—until a new man, Alfred Pendlebury (Stanley Holloway), turns up at his lodgings. Pendlebury owns a small foundry making cheap lead souvenirs (such as Eiffel Towers) and Holland realizes this is the perfect cover for smuggling the gold abroad. Pendlebury, who also has his dreams—he is a sculptor in his spare time and is fond of literary quotations—quickly agrees and they team up with two professional criminals (Sid

◀

An enduringly funny British film, it was made at Ealing Studios during the studio's golden period from 1947 to 1955.

James and Alfie Bass) to help realize the scheme. The heist is carried out as planned but in Paris a misunderstanding with a retailer leads to six gold Eiffel Tower models being sold to a party of British schoolgirls. From this point the film becomes a chase caper. After more setbacks they eventually recover all the models but in doing so alert the police, and a pursuit ensues, until Pendlebury is finally caught, while Holland escapes.

"BY JOVE, HOLLAND, IT'S A GOOD JOB WE'RE HONEST MEN."

ALFRED PENDLEBURY

As Charles Barr points out, *The Lavender Hill Mob* can be grouped with other Ealing comedies *Whisky Galore!* (1949) and *Kind Hearts and Coronets* (1949) as wish-fulfillment films, appealing to viewers' secret fantasies: "Their conventionally moral resolutions are imposed in a tongue-in-cheek way, right at the end, without challenging our commitment to their central characters' single-minded projects or even our belief that they really got away with it successfully." Indeed, at the end of the movie in Rio, where we discover that Holland is handcuffed to a policeman ready to take him back to England and to jail, he is pleased that he at least got a year of living his dream.

Other notable features include an early appearance by Audrey Hepburn in a small role near the start; and the fact that director Charles Crichton made a remarkable comeback at age seventy eight with *A Fish Called Wanda* in 1988. **KM**

► **Potential millionaire Henry Holland (Guinness) is tied up.**

THE BIG HEAT 1953 (U.S.)

Director Fritz Lang **Producer** Robert Arthur **Screenplay** Sydney Boehm, William P. McGivern (based on the novel) **Cinematography** Charles Lang **Music** Daniele Amfitheatrof, Arthur Morton, Henry Vars **Cast** Glenn Ford, Gloria Grahame, Jocelyn Brando, Lee Marvin, Alexander Scourby, Jeanette Nolan

Next to *Rancho Notorious* (1952), *The Big Heat* is possibly Fritz Lang's most famous Hollywood film; a gritty and surprisingly violent crime thriller of political corruption and vengeance. Detective Dave Bannion (Ford) is the one honest cop in a city filled with corruption. Investigating the apparent suicide of a fellow cop that just doesn't smell right to him, Bannion begins to upset the applecart of criminal payoffs when he begins investigating "businessman" Mike Lagana (Scourby). Bannion is warned off from investigating Lagana, but pays no heed, resulting in his wife being blown up in a car bomb meant for him. While on compassionate leave from the force, Bannion continues his investigation personally—what one character refers to as a "hate binge," which is an imaginative euphemism for revenge. One of Lagana's hoodlums, a psychotic young hood named Vince (Marvin), becomes Bannion's chief nemesis. Vince's mouthy moll, Debby (Grahame), is permanently scarred by the gangster with a pot of boiling coffee thrown in her face in one of the film's most notorious moments. It is this act that turns Debby away from Vince and she begins spilling the beans to Bannion in her own "hate binge."

◄
This movie struck a new note of realism in the potrayal of violence in crime films, and was much condemned on its release.

Lang strips down William P. McGivern's book to its bare bones, providing the story with a narrative drive as efficient and devastating as a handgun. Every scene is constructed with economy—the dialogue is functional and concise, and the action is never gratuitous. Today it is as easy for us to find McCarthyism in the films of this period as it was for McCarthyites to find evidence of Communist infiltration back in the 1950s.

"WELL, YOU'RE ABOUT AS ROMANTIC AS A PAIR OF HANDCUFFS."

DEBBY MARSH

However, *The Big Heat* does seem particularly appropriate for having McCarthyite ideology read into it. Throughout the picture, no one wants to talk to Bannion; despite the claimed sympathy for the loss of his wife, he is stonewalled at every step of his investigation. Everyone in the city seems to be covering up the truth out of fear of reprisals from Lagana. The key comes from the bravery of a crippled secretary who feels that "what's right is right," who testifies against the crooks once she knows whom to tell. Once people start informing on Lagana, his entire empire begins to crumble and American justice can finally be served. Although certainly *The Big Heat* is not as in-your-face as Kazan's self-apology, *On the Waterfront* (1954), Lang's film fundamentally serves the same ideology, namely that it is only once a few brave individuals begin to turn "stoolie" that the criminals (read Communists) will be brought to justice. **MK**

► Glenn Ford gave one of his most typical performances as Detective Dave Bannion, seen here apprehending psychopathic gangster Vince (Marvin).

Allied Artists presents

CORNEL · RICHARD · BRIAN · JEAN
WILDE · CONTE · DONLEVY · WALLACE

THE MOST STARTLING STORY THE SCREEN HAS EVER DARED REVEAL!

THE BIG COMBO

Written by PHILIP YORDAN · Produced by SIDNEY HARMON · Directed by JOSEPH LEWIS

THE BIG COMBO 1955 (U.S.)

Director Joseph. H. Lewis **Producer** Sidney Harmon **Screenplay** Philip Yordan
Cinematography John Alton **Music** David Raksin **Cast** Cornel Wilde, Richard Conte,
Brian Donlevy, Jean Wallace, Lee Van Cleef, Earl Holliman, Helen Walker, Jay Adler,
John Hoyt, Ted de Corsia, Helene Stanton, Roy Gordon, Steve Mitchell, Baynes Barron

By 1955, late in the classic cycle, film noir had only two ways
to go. It could go *grise*, softening its edges and toning down
its excesses; or it could go baroque, embracing its hard-edged
cynicism and surrendering to those features that had always
made it fit uneasily into the array of Hollywood genres.

In 1955, there wasn't much noir had to say that was genuinely
new; audiences knew its tone and outlook. Earlier post-war
noirs had already demonstrated its continued relevance to a
more upbeat post-war America. In its baroque incarnation, even
noir's most accomplished practitioners could get down and
dirty. Noir was finally freed from all residual claims social realism
might have had on it; it could now devote itself to creating and
detailing an overtly artificial universe of nastiness. Visual style,
turned by cinematographers into a lovingly cultivated fetish,
was the way either to bid farewell to substance, or to erase the
difference between style and substance altogether.

On the least interesting level, *The Big Combo* is the story of a
gangster and the cop obsessed with bringing him down.
Getting ground up in the power struggle between them is, of
course, a woman. The usual suspects populate the cast of

◀

**Actors Cornel Wilde
and Jean Wallace
married in 1951,
and their marriage
lasted for 30
years before they
divorced in 1981.**

minor characters: two hoods living in near matrimonial harmony, a second-in-command of the criminal organization that lends the film its title, and an assortment of cops and underworld characters. Bits and pieces of this story are borrowed from the American Manual of Noir: there's a Swede, and a man patiently awaiting his own assassination; and in the end, the once-great Mr. Brown (Conte) goes down for his crimes

"KILLING IS VERY PERSONAL. ONCE IT GETS STARTED, IT'S HARD TO STOP."

MR. BROWN

just in time, thanks to the Breen Office—like Robinson, Cagney, and Bogart in every other Warner Bros. picture from the 1930s. Although plot and character hardly rise above the level of pure genre, style is everything here. Unburdened by the dictates of narrative originality, cinematographer John Alton is in charge. Unlike classic noirs, in which expressionistic style is commonly reserved for showy set pieces, *The Big Combo* is visually intense, worked over, polished, and tweaked in virtually every scene. Alton's tireless visual inventiveness not only covers up the cheapness of the production, but at times seems capable of divorcing imagery from content altogether. The showdown in the closing scene is an all-chiaroscuro version of the final shot of *Casablanca*. There is nothing new here about organized crime or justice, but what Alton can do with a few key lights and a fog machine is worth watching for alone. **SH**

► Mr. Brown (Conte) tortures Lt. Diamond (Wilde) assisted by Fante (Van Cleef) in one of the movie's several ugly torture scenes.

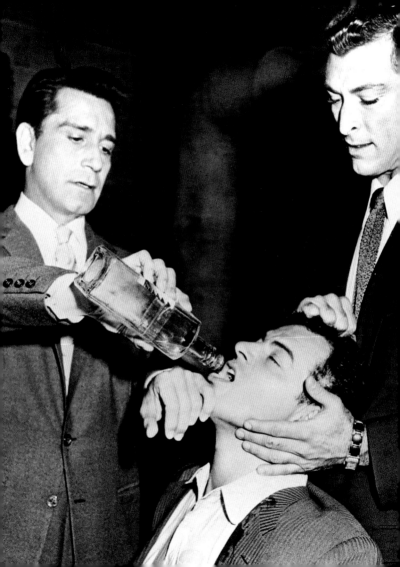

RIFIFI 1955 (FRANCE)

Director Jules Dassin **Producer** René Gaston Vuattoux **Screenplay** René Wheeler, Jules Dassin, Auguste Le Breton (from the novel by Auguste Le Breton) **Cinematography** Philippe Agostini **Music** Georges Auric **Cast** Jean Servais, Pierre Grasset, Carl Möhner, Robert Manuel, Claude Sylvain, Janine Darcey, Robert Hossein

The greatest of all heist movies, *Rififi*—which is French criminal slang for "trouble"—has had many imitators that use "Rififi" in their title, but Jules Dassin's film is the original.

Tony Le Stéphanois (Servais) has just been released from prison, much aged and with a worrisome cough that could be a sign of tuberculosis. He may want to go straight, but he knows little besides the criminal underworld. His girlfriend has moved on and is now the main squeeze of flashy nightclub owner Louis Grutter (Grasset). There is only one thing Le Stéphanois can do: put together a new crew and pull off one last heist so daring and big that the proceeds will enable him to live out his last few years in relative comfort. Human nature being what it is, once the heist has been pulled with relative ease, mistakes get made, and Grutter is on the trail of the burglars so he can cash in on the reward money. Grutter also suspects that Le Stéphanois is involved in the heist, and ratting him out will get rid of his rival once and for all.

At the center of *Rififi* is the thirty-minute heist sequence filmed almost entirely in silence because of the criminals trying to avoid setting off the alarm. It is one of the singular most

◄

The screenplay is extracted from an Auguste Le Breton novel. Legend has it that the author was so angry at the cuts that he drew a pistol on Dassin, who responded with laughter.

remarkable sequences of suspense in European cinema, and in terms of construction, editing, and execution, ranks up there with the Odessa Steps sequence from Eisenstein's *Battleship Potemkin* (1925) as a landmark moment of pure cinema. This is despite Dassin's claim that the reason so much of the film is told visually was because of his poor French. Beyond the surface gloss of the film is a poetic portrait of Le Stéphanois, a

"YOU'RE NOT THE ONLY ONE THAT HAD AN UNHAPPY CHILDHOOD."

LOUISE LE SUEDOIS

professional thief who knows he is going to die soon. Once Grutter murders gang member Mario (Manuel) and Mario's wife, Ida (Sylvain), and kidnaps his best friend Jo's (Möhner) young son, Le Stéphanois becomes a lone antihero out for revenge, and his attempt to rescue the boy is the man's one last chance to try to redeem himself. Although not quite a throwback to French pre-war poetic realism, Dassin is able to evoke a gritty, poetic variation to the ubiquitous vengeance plot.

Dassin himself plays the dandified thief, Cesar. He had originally come to Hollywood in 1940 serving as apprentice director to Alfred Hitchcock and Garson Kanin. By refusing to testify at the House Un-American Activities Committee in 1952 he was blacklisted—ending his Hollywood career. He moved to Paris in 1953 where despite his lack of French, he made *Rififi* and won Best Director at the 1955 Cannes Film Festival. **MK**

►
Tony (Servais) with the tied-up Cesar (Dassin). This scene was included to echo how Dassin felt after being betrayed by his contemporaries. in America.

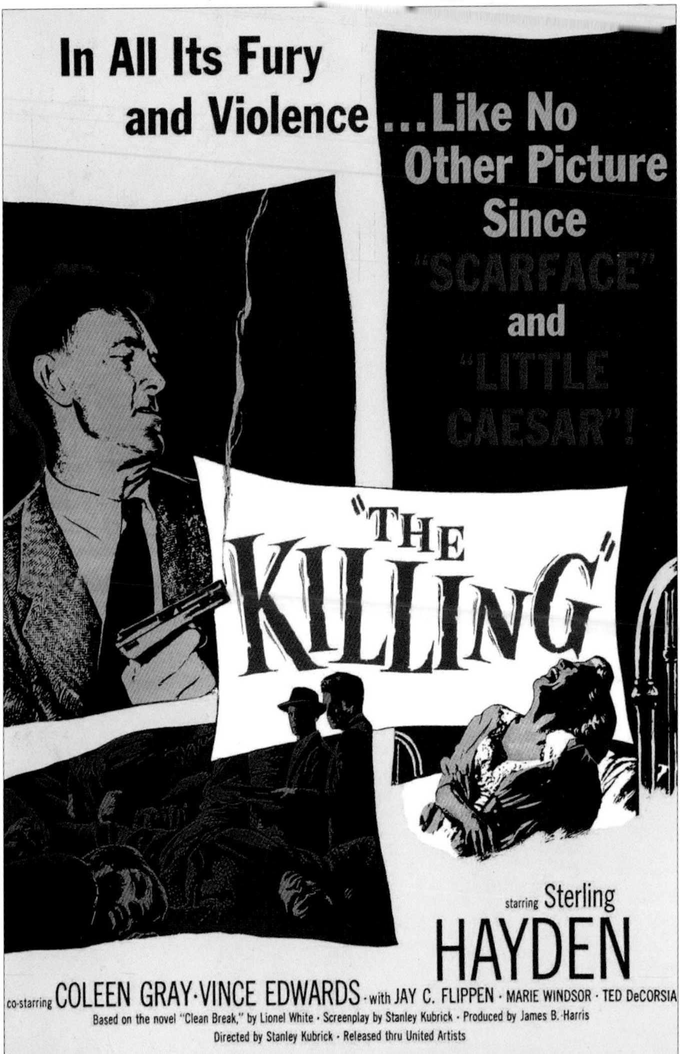
In All Its Fury
and Violence ...Like No
Other Picture
Since
"SCARFACE"
and
"LITTLE
CAESAR"!
"THE KILLING"
starring Sterling
HAYDEN
co-starring COLEEN GRAY · VINCE EDWARDS · with JAY C. FLIPPEN · MARIE WINDSOR · TED DeCORSIA
Based on the novel "Clean Break," by Lionel White · Screenplay by Stanley Kubrick · Produced by James B. Harris
Directed by Stanley Kubrick · Released thru United Artists

THE KILLING 1956 (U.S.)

Director Stanley Kubrick **Producer** James B. Harris **Screenplay** Stanley Kubrick, Jim Thompson (dialogue) (from the novel *Clean Break* by Lionel White) **Cinematography** Lucien Ballard **Music** Gerald Fried **Cast** Sterling Hayden, Marie Windsor, Vince Edwards, Coleen Gray, Jay C. Flippen, Timothy Carey, Joe Sawyer

Decades before Quentin Tarantino made nonlinear storytelling fashionable in crime cinema, *The Killing* told a heist-gone-wrong story with the structure of a complex jigsaw puzzle, and the naturalistic style of a factual documentary.

Small-time crook Johnny Clay (Hayden) wants to pull off one big job before retiring. He assembles a crew and they meticulously design the robbery of a racetrack. Beyond expectations, the heist succeeds. But when the gang meets to divide the money, they find they have been betrayed by one gang member's wife (Windsor), and her lover (Edwards). In the ensuing shoot-outs everyone perishes, except Johnny. He and his wife (Gray) manage to make it to the airport. Right before they board their plane, however, a freak occurrence on the runway causes their suitcase to open up, scattering their loot, and their hopes, in the wind.

The quality of *The Killing* lies not in its story, but in its expository tone, structure, and atmosphere. Everything leading up to the heist is told like a documentary investigation, including a detached staccato voice-over, location shooting (the San Francisco Golden Gate racetrack), and an abundance

◄

Kubrick's first full-length feature film was his first collaboration with young producer James B. Harris. They worked together on Kubrick's next three films.

of trivia only a courtroom would pay attention to ("At exactly three forty five on that Saturday afternoon in the last week of September . . . ," the movie's first lines go). To that is added a structure that mixes up the chronology to augment suspense, and an omniscient narration leads us through the story, revealing facts out of sequence. On top of that *The Killing* is drenched in a sense of foreboding, a "predetermined final

"THE BIGGEST MISTAKE I MADE BEFORE WAS SHOOTING FOR PEANUTS."

JOHNNY CLAY

design," as one character calls it. The result is a chess game that treats characters like pawns (something Kubrick would become known for), a film that focuses on the inventiveness of the scheme instead of on the plot resolution, robbing the viewer of any hope while keeping the tensions high.

The Killing received extensive praise from critics of the time as a refreshing and innovative picture. Much of that praise went to Kubrick. But the film is equally the child of producer James B. Harris. After *The Killing*, Kubrick left the gangster movie behind him. But Harris returned to the genre to write the screenplay for *Boiling Point* (1993), and to produce *Cop* (1988) and *The Black Dahlia* (2006), based on the work of hard-boiled novelist James Ellroy. Today, *The Killing* is widely seen as the film that inspired *Reservoir Dogs* (1992) and *Pulp Fiction* (1994) in blending a detached tone and complex story structures. **EM**

▶
Bartender Mike O'Reilly (Sawyer), eyeballs this delightfully wrapped box, which is unlikely to contain flowers he can take home to Mother.

BOB LE FLAMBEUR 1956 (FRANCE)

Director Jean-Pierre Melville **Producers** Jean-Pierre Melville and Serge Silberman
Screenplay Auguste Le Breton, Jean-Pierre Melville **Cinematography** Henri Decaë
Music Eddie Barclay, Jo Boyer **Cast** Roger Duchesne, Isabelle Corey, Daniel Cauchy,
André Garet, Gérard Buhr, Guy Decomble, Claude Cerval, Howard Vernon, Colette Fleury

Bob le Flambeur (a.k.a. *Fever Heat*)—which translates as "Bob the
Gambler"—was the first gangster film from French director
Jean-Pierre Melville, who would go on to make a series of
spartan, bleak gangster movies, among them *Le Samouraï*
(1967), *Le Cercle Rouge* (1970), and *Un Flic* (1972). By contrast, *Bob
le Flambeur* is a lighter, if still melancholic, affair. Bob Montagné
(Duchesne) is a well-known figure in Montmartre whose
criminal activities are long behind him. He is friendly with the
local police, and the unnamed narrator—voiced by Melville
himself—describes him as "that aging young man." The plot
into which he is drawn turns out to be both conventional and
negligible. A run of bad luck at gambling leaves Bob broke, so
he forms a team to rob a casino. Inevitably he is betrayed—by
women in a film that, for all its virtues, is rife with a casual
misogyny—and is arrested by his policeman friend.

Melville is clearly not that interested in the opportunities for
suspense offered by such a scenario, concentrating instead on
detailing Bob's Montmartre milieu—and in so doing provides a
sensitive portrayal of the aging gangster. The film begins
atmospherically by following the silver-haired Bob through the

◄

**An ironic French
take on the noir
genre that is dark
in subject but
lighter in tone,
exposing the
weaknesses that
dog humanity.**

streets of Montmartre early one morning. Although he is clearly known and respected by all, Melville manages to convey a sense both of his isolation and of an emotional impairment. He lives alone in a bare, impersonal flat where the sole personal fixture is a slot machine, and his only meaningful relationships seem to be with Paolo (Cauchy), the son of an old friend to whom he acts as a father figure, and the local police inspector.

"MONTMARTRE IS BOTH HEAVEN AND HELL."

JEAN-PIERRE MELVILLE

Despite this, he involves Paulo in his attempted robbery and shows little response to Paolo's death at the hands of a group of police led by the police inspector.

In a conclusion replete with irony, Bob, who is a compulsive gambler, embarks on an extraordinary run of luck while in the casino waiting for the raid to begin. This results both in his winning a large amount of cash and in his neglecting his duties in the robbery and thereby contributing to its failure. The picture ends with Bob speculating humorously on whether he can use his winnings to hire a lawyer who will get him off the charges he will face. Yet in the meantime Paolo has died and the aging Bob is alone again. By Melville's bleak standards, it is a happy ending, but elements of bitterness lurk just beneath the surface. This is a wonderfully shot film that captures to perfection the moody atmosphere of a shadowy Paris. **PH**

► **Roger Duchesne in the title role— strikingly similar to Burt Lancaster's role in *Atlantic City* a quarter of a century later.**

TOUCH OF EVIL 1958 (U.S.)

Director Orson Welles **Producer** Albert Zugsmith **Screenplay** Orson Welles
(from the novel *Badge of Evil* by Whit Masterson) **Cinematography** Russell Metty
Music Henry Mancini **Cast** Charlton Heston, Janet Leigh, Orson Welles, Joseph Calleia,
Zsa Zsa Gabor, Marlene Dietrich, Akim Tamiroff, Joanna Moore, Ray Collins, Mort Mills

Orson Welles often avoided genres, but *Touch of Evil* fully
embraces the treats of the gangster movie. More so, with its
depictions of police corruption, Mafia crime, drug trafficking,
and gang violence, it puts the entire model of the genre into
one film, shakes it up, and reinvents it.

The story centers on two police officers battling it out
against the backdrop of Mafia crime in a U.S.-Mexican border
town. The impeccable Mexican agent Vargas (Heston) suspects
that the sleazy, addicted American cop Quinlan (Welles) is
fabricating evidence about the assassination of a wealthy
businessman. To protect his reputation, Quinlan arranges to
have Vargas' bride, Susie (Leigh), kidnapped, drugged, and
raped. He also frames the family of the drug lord Grandi (who
has previously threatened Vargas) and has them rounded up in
order to reap the rewards. But he is found out and confronted
by his protégé Menzies (Calleia). Quinlan kills Menzies, but the
murder, and his confession, are taped. In a fight over the tape
Vargas kills Quinlan—the new order replacing the old.

Stylistically, *Touch of Evil* plays in a league all its own. Often
style comes at the expense of storytelling, but not so here.

◄
**As actor and
director, Welles'
presence
dominates this
movie—the stories
of his involvement
could make a film
by themselves.**

A good example is the dazzling opening shot, which is quite simply one of the most daring pieces of filmmaking that has ever been made. Supported by a brilliant jazz score, the three-and-a-half-minute continuous tracking shot encapsulates all that cinema has to offer. At the same time it gives crucial plot information and sets the pace for a breakneck story. Amidst the bravura, the supporting cast is fabulous, especially the faded

"YOU KNOW WHAT'S WRONG WITH YOU? YOU'VE BEEN SEEING TOO MANY GANGSTER MOVIES." *SUSIE VARGAS*

glory of Quinlan's old flame Tanya (Dietrich), the socialite strip-club owner (Gabor), and the various hipsters, gangs, and mobs (one of them led by a butch Mercedes McCambridge).

The history surrounding *Touch of Evil* is a story in itself. Welles developed various shady ways to shield the production from interference by Universal studios—comparisons with the fly-by-night operations in the film are hard to avoid. Universal still took the editing out of Welles' hands. In the 1970s, a so-called "preview cut" became a cult hit, and in the 1990s, after a furious memo about the cuts by Welles was unearthed, *Touch of Evil* was re-released in its intended format. Regardless of the confusion around the various versions, however, *Touch of Evil*'s bold style and hard-boiled story about a fading old West being replaced by a modern world where there is no longer room for any Quinlans (or Welleses) make it a definitive gangster movie. **EM**

► Honest cop Vargas (Heston) finds that his wife (Leigh) becomes a target in this sweaty tale of corruption.

AL CAPONE 1959 (U.S.)

Director Richard Wilson **Producers** Leonard J. Ackerman, John H. Burrows
Screenplay Malvin Wald, Henry F. Greenberg **Cinematography** Lucien Ballard
Music David Raksin **Cast** Rod Steiger, Fay Spain, James Gregory, Martin Balsam,
Nehemiah Persoff, Murvyn Vye, Robert Gist, Lewis Charles, Joe De Santis

Rod Steiger is the big screen's first "method mobster," and the primary reason to check out this well-made if otherwise undistinguished biopic of America's most iconic gangster. The picture gets underway quickly with the Brooklyn hood's arrival in Chicago on the eve of Prohibition. Old pal Johnny Torrio (Persoff) invites him to be his right-hand man, and soon enough the ambitious Capone has persuaded "Johnny Papa" that they should do away with their opera-loving boss, Big Jim Colosimo (De Santis) and divvy up the Chicago streets with Dion O'Banion (Gist), "Hymie" Weiss (Charles), and "Bugs" Moran (Vye).

As written by Malvin Wald (*The Naked City* [1948]) and Henry F. Greenberg, and directed by Orson Welles' protégé Richard Wilson, the film hits just about all the high points of Capone's infamous career. Moreover, it does an admirable job of revealing the backstage of Chicago's political corruption in which different gangs competed to take control of one of the biggest cities in America. When taking into consideration the date of the movie's release, there are some very violent scenes on display here, such as the Saint Valentine's Day Massacre sequence and other showdowns between the gangsters.

◄

Bordering on caricature, Rod Steiger holds the audience with his masterly impersonation of the Chicago hoodlum.

Wilson directs the story masterfully, utilizing a very crisp tempo, especially for the action scenes. Stylistically, as shot through the lens of cinematographer Lucien Ballard (who later worked on Budd Boetticher's 1960 gangster classic *The Rise and Fall of Legs Diamond*), *Al Capone* arguably set the mold for the T.V. series *The Untouchables*, destined to make pop-culture history just three years later. (It is also worth noting here that

"YOU CAN GO [FAR] WITH A SMILE. YOU CAN GO A LOT FARTHER WITH A SMILE AND A GUN." *ATTRIBUTED TO AL CAPONE*

Persoff had a recurring role on the series, playing, among other parts, Capone's bookkeeper, "Greasy Thumbs" Guzik.) In an early starring role, Steiger delivers every line with maniacal zest—as if it might be his last. He is given multiple shades and layers of character, a sense of humility as he ingratiates himself with the bosses, a sense of intelligence as he tries to asses each of his rival's strengths and vulnerabilities, as well as a sense of shrewdness as he attermpts to get his way through charm or brute force. As film reviewer Richard T. Jameson has pointed out, "there are even uncanny moments (and this, of course, is pure accident—or is it, in fact, mythic rightness) when you would swear you could glimpse the once and future Tony Soprano." And in a nod to the Production Code in effect then, although the real Al Capone died of advanced syphilis, the narrator attributes Capone's death to an unnamed "incurable disease." **KW**

► **Shades of Tony Soprano—Rod Steiger in full flow with a clever performance as the larger-than-life mobster.**

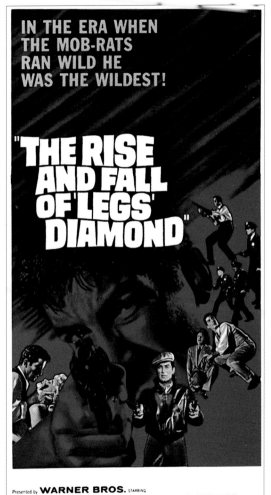

IN THE ERA WHEN
THE MOB-RATS
RAN WILD HE
WAS THE WILDEST!

"THE RISE
AND FALL
OF 'LEGS'
DIAMOND"

Presented by **WARNER BROS.** STARRING
RAY DANTON · KAREN STEELE · ELAINE STEWART
Written by JOSEPH LANDON · A UNITED STATES PRODUCTIONS PICTURE
Music by
LEONARD ROSENMAN
Produced by MILTON SPERLING · Directed by BUDD BOETTICHER

THE RISE AND FALL
OF LEGS DIAMOND 1960 (U.S.)

Director Budd Boetticher **Screenplay** Joseph Landon **Producer** Leon Chooluck, Milton Sperling **Cinematography** Lucien Ballard **Music** Leonard Rosenman **Cast** Ray Danton, Karen Steele, Elaine Stewart, Jesse White, Simon Oakland, Robert Lowery, Judson Pratt, Warren Oates, Frank DeKova, Gordon Jones, Joseph Ruskin

A film like a dance—choreographed, elegant, and elegiac—this is the story of Jack Diamond (Danton), known as "Legs," a talented stepper and cheap hoodlum. He's a lowlife with high-flying ambitions, acting ruthlessly and relentlessly to achieve his goals. Verging on psychopathy, he cares only about himself, doing anything—including killing in cold blood anybody who stands in his way—to reach the top. His big idea is to move in on the operations of Mob boss Arnold Rothstein (Lowery). However, getting there is not only a question of bloodshed and brutality, but of tricks and tactics as well.

All of Budd Boetticher's films are essentially films about the corrida. He was a matador himself before coming to Hollywood as a consultant for bullfighting movies, assisting Rouben Mamoulian and later realizing his notional life story (*The Bullfighter and the Lady* [1951]). Boetticher's westerns, often starring Randolph Scott, operate as corrida films, too, featuring laconic plots that openly emphasize their constructed nature. His heroes play with their enemies just as the torero does with

◄

Inspired by the TV success of *The Untouchables*, this film was part of a brief attempt by Warner Bros. to recapture its pre-war "gangster" image.

the bull; they provoke and irritate them in order to entice them into improvident reactions as reluctance always leads to failure. Mobster Legs Diamond is a master of this manipulative game as well, but in the end he fails because of his narcissistic selfishness and opportunism—which are his greatest strengths and weaknesses simultaneously. The last line of the movie sums it all up: "He never loved anybody; that's why he's dead."

"DIAMOND WAS A SON OF A BITCH, PROBABLY THE WORST MAN WHO EVER LIVED!" BUDD BOETTICHER

Seeing this picture it inevitably becomes clear that the gangster film is not a subgenre of the crime movie, but of comedy. The film's violence owes more to Chaplin and Lubitsch than to Aldrich or Fuller; it turns out as solid slapstick par excellence. While Legs Diamond piles up one corpse after another, it's obvious that Boetticher aims not for serious tragedy but for a sarcastic satire of Hollywood's glamorous success story. In Boetticher's perversely dark vision of America, only a killer can come off. His Legs Diamond, as brilliantly played by a slick Ray Danton, is a bizarre creature, simultaneously hyena and hawk, a fallen angel hell-bent on emerging from the crowd. In a pitch-black, ironic ending Diamond's success turns into failure not because of police action, but because of a new kind of gangster who operates in a seemingly legal manner—rejecting his own, antiquated methods. He suddenly is nothing—again. **IR**

► Ray Danton in his most celebrated role as the vicious prohibition gangster Jack "Legs" Diamond.

THE 1000 EYES OF DR. MABUSE

1960 (FRANCE • ITALY • WEST GERMANY)

Director Fritz Lang **Producers** Artur Brauner, Fritz Lang **Screenplay** Fritz Lang, Heinz Oskar Wuttig **Cinematography** Karl Löb **Music** Gerhard Becker, Bert Grund **Cast** Peter Van Eyck, Gert Fröbe, Wolfgang Preiss, Werner Peters, Andrea Checchi, Howard Vernon, Nico Pepe, David Cameron, Dawn Addams, Jean-Jacques Delbo

While Fritz Lang's public image as a genius auteur remained surprisingly untarnished after he left Germany in 1933, American audiences, critics, and industry insiders often turned a cold shoulder. Lang returned from Hollywood to post-war Germany in the late 1950s, trying to reconnect with his former glory returning to tried and tested properties. After remaking Joe May's silent 1921 adventure The *Indian Tomb* in 1959, Lang revived a character that had helped to establish his reputation. *The 1000 Eyes of Dr. Mabuse* was to be his final film; like much of his work, it is a mixed bag of mediocrity and greatness.

The picture reconnects the star director with his star creation: Dr. Mabuse (admirably played by Wolfgang Preiss), the mad genius of crime, bent on plunging the world into anarchy from which a new Nietzschean order will emerge. Lang had plucked Mabuse, the creation of pulp writer Norbert Jacques, out of a pool of cartoonish mastermind criminals. Lang elevated him, in two brilliantly inventive, visually innovative pre-war thrillers (*Dr. Mabuse, the Gambler* [1922], *The Testament of Dr. Mabuse* [1933]), from his lowly origins in pulp fiction to a key metaphor

◀

Veteran director Fritz Lang's last film is a supremely elborate thriller where nothing is quite what it seems.

for the political and economic chaos of late Weimar. Applying the formula, introduced first in *Testament*, of yet another madman taking his inspiration and name from the original Mabuse, Lang establishes his villain as a credible force in the world of post-war Germany. Shielding cold-blooded economic and political calculation behind supernatural spectacle, Mabuse and his network of agents undermine the economic and

"THE MOST DANGEROUS CRIMINAL OF ALL TIME BACK AT WORK? THIS FILM PROVIDES THE ANSWER!" *TAGLINE*

political stability of the post-war world. As the film's title suggests, surveillance is omnipresent, whether through cameras, telescopes, or one-way mirrors. Yet Mabuse is not the sole creator of this paranoid pan–optic society; his nemesis in the police force, Inspector Kras (Fröbe), is equally invested in the omnipresence of surveillance.

Constantly alluding to his two earlier *Mabuse* films, Lang tries to maneuver past the weaknesses of the Gothic claptrap he inherits, wittingly or not, from a staff and minor cast employed regularly in the Edgar Wallace *krimis* popular in Germany during the late 1950s and '60s. More than the campy films of that franchise, however, Lang's film did strike a chord; a string of seven new *Mabuse* films in the wake of *1000 Eyes* testifies to a suspicion that, underneath the slick post-war surfaces, the new Europe looked a lot like its Weimar precursor. **SH**

►
Murders in a Berlin hotel equipped with surveillance in every room are suspected to be the work of the reincarnated criminal genius Dr. Mabuse.

UNDERWORLD U.S.A 1961 (U.S.)

Director Samuel Fuller **Producer** Samuel Fuller **Screenplay** Samuel Fuller
Cinematography Hal Mohr **Music** Harry Sukman **Cast** Cliff Robertson, Dolores
Dorn, Beatrice Kay, Paul Dubov, Robert Emhardt, Larry Gates, Richard Rust, Gerald
Milton, Allan Gruener, David Kent, Tina Pine, Sally Mills, Robert P. Lieb, Neyle Morrow

This is a movie like a catchphrase: striking, succinct,
sententious. This is a movie that is not aiming for a smooth,
classical continuity, but for a sequence of savage sensations.
Every cut is an act of violence. "Film is like a battleground,"
says director Samuel Fuller. "Love. Hate. Action. Violence. And
death. In one word: Emotion." Affects are what Fuller's cinema
essentially is about, wanting to have a sentimental influence
on the viewer as straight and squarely as possible.

   Fuller's cinema is characterized by the two most important
experiences of his life—his work as a crime and court reporter
on the one hand, and his years of being a foot soldier in World
War II on the other. They come together in *Underworld U.S.A.*,
which is based on a series of articles about organized crime in
the *Saturday Evening Post* and conceives the gangster film as a
war movie. In Fuller's films, war functions as daily routine—a
natural process of urban life. Therefore, to live means trying to
survive in a world of bleakness, without any clearly drawn lines.

   Underworld U.S.A. starts with pictures of pitch-black
shadows on a back-alley wall showing a murder. These
shadows never let go of Tolly Devlin (Robertson), a teenage

◄
**Fuller subverts
the gangster genre
by transforming it
into another—war.
The battleground
is America, the
pugilists the FBI
and the Syndicate.**

punk forced to witness the killing of his old man. Obsessed with the idea of revenge he spends the next twenty years planning his vengeance, even going to far as to go to jail just to have the opportunity to learn the names of the murderers. Devlin is a far cry from the American hero, blind and brutal, selfish and savage, disloyal and degenerate—a bitter farewell to the tradition of altruism. Fuller delights in framing him in

"THIS IS DIRECT CINEMA, UNCRITICIZABLE, IRREPROACHABLE, 'GIVEN' CINEMA." FRANÇOIS TRUFFAUT

tight close-ups, emphasizing the fanatic relentlessness beneath his boyish good looks. He is a ruthless killer just like the men he lives to kill.

The Mobsters in *Underworld U.S.A.* no longer operate as small-time crooks but as taxpaying citizens. They are wealthy businessmen, senior staff owned by arithmetic and accountancy. The underworld in America is nothing else than the world of executives. Thus Fuller breaks the mold of the genre's romantic vision of the gangster as tragic hero. Only Devlin's edgy energy and restless ruckus still remind us of the great mythic gangster figures in the past. But it is an energy and ruckus that is carrying us toward death. The movie ends how and where it began, with a death in the urban backyards, in a dirty little lane. There the shadows dominate the light, and all white is absorbed in black. **IR**

▶
The graphic visual image with which the movie starts and ends is iconic.

BRANDED TO KILL 1967 (JAPAN)

Director Seijun Suzuki **Producer** Kaneo Iwai, Takiko Mizunoe **Screenplay** Hachiro
Guryu, Takeo Kimura, Chusei Sone, Atsushi Yamatoya **Cinematography** Kazue
Nagatsuka **Music** Naozumi Yamamoto **Cast** Jo Shishido, Mariko Ogawa, Anne
Mari, Koji Nambara, Isao Tamagawa, Hiroshi Minami, Iwae Arai, Kosuke Hisamatsu

A prolific filmmaker, Seijun Suzuki came to fame as a director of
B movies for the major Japanese studio Nikkatsu. However,
Branded to Kill, which is now seen as one of Suzuki's finest
pictures, led to an acrimonious parting of the ways when
Nikkatsu—horrified at what they saw as an incomprehensible
film unlikely to make money—fired the director. Suzuki
successfully sued Nikkatsu for breach of contract, but found
himself blacklisted for over ten years as a result. Shot in just 25
days, with one week pre-production and three days allowed for
post-production—necessitated by Nikkatsu's intense schedule
—*Branded to Kill* fits loosely into the yakuza genre. With their
stringent code of honor and emphasis on morality or *ninkyo*
(chivalry), early yakuza films were popular escapes in Japan at
the height of the so-called "economic miracle." In the late 1960s,
a genre of yakuza film appeared concerned with showing the
reality of the underworld: the *jitsuroku* (true-life document).
In *Branded to Kill*, guns, knives, and needles replace the
compulsory *kanata* sword of the *ninkyo* (chivalry film) genre.
The defiant yakuza defending the nation's honor against the
invasion of Western capitalism is transformed into Killer

◀

**Contract Director
Suzuki specialized
in movies catering
to rebellious youth
audiences, his
films becoming
increasingly
anarchic during
the 1960s.**

Number 3, whose mission in life seems to be merely to proceed up the ranks. Early in the film, he sets Number 2 on fire before cleanly dispatching Number 4. Although this should ensure a rise up the ranks, Hanada fails to successfully complete a hit ordered by the Head of the Yakuza, and so becomes a marked man himself. The climactic sequences in the deserted wrestling hall, when Number 1 attempts to kill Hanada but ends up

"WHERE IS NUMBER ONE? I KNOW HE'S AIMING AT ME."

JO SHISHIDO (KILLER NUMBER 3)

being killed himself, might at first suggest that Hanada is now Number 1. However, this comes at a price, as he then mistakenly kills the woman with whom he has fallen in love.

If thin on plot, the film is heavy on style. Shot in monochrome, *Branded to Kill* is a nonstop visual and aural assault on the senses and is the first film to feature a first-person shooter sequence. The emphasis on the immediacy of the senses situates *Branded to Kill* in the Japanese New Wave. Like many characters in films of New Wave directors, Hanada is defined by his animal appetites—his strange proclivity for boiled rice; the violent couplings with his wife; and his attraction to the masochistic femme fatale Misako (Mari). This emphasis on extreme bodily passions is not surprising, taking into account the fact that Suzuki's earlier *Market of Flesh* (1964) is often cited as one of the earliest Japanese pink films (*pinku eiga*). **CBa**

► Jo Shishido with gun and bikini-clad babe. The influence of James Bond features strongly in the look of many Japanese pop yakuza noir movies of this period.

A WARNING! This motion picture depicts without flinching the most shocking event of America's most lawless era…The St. Valentine's Day Massacre!

20th Century-Fox Presents

THE ST. VALENTINE'S DAY MASSACRE!

Suggested For Mature Audiences

Starring
Jason Robards, George Segal, Ralph Meeker, Jean Hale
Produced and directed by Roger Corman · Written by Howard Browne · Panavision® Color by DeLuxe

THE ST. VALENTINE'S DAY MASSACRE 1967 (U.S.)

Director Roger Corman **Producer** Roger Corman **Screenplay** Howard Browne **Cinematography** Milton R. Krasner **Music** Lionel Newman, Fred Steiner **Cast** Jason Robards, George Segal, Ralph Meeker, Jean Hale, Clint Ritchie, Frank Silvera, Michele Guarini, Alexander D'Arcy, Richard Bakalyan, David Canary

One of Roger Corman's few big-budget, major studio films, *The St. Valentine's Day Massacre* purports to re-create the gangster massacre of February 14, 1929, in Chicago exactly as it happened. Driven by a Welles-style narration that never tires in its detailed explanations of character backgrounds, allegiances, and fate, the result is a docudrama that chronicles the massacre and key incidents leading up to it.

The long-standing territorial feud between Bugs Moran's (Meeker) north-side Irish outfit and Al Capone's (Robards) south-side Italian Mob comes to a head when Capone enlists the up-and-coming Jack McGurn (Ritchie), who goes to work devising a plan to wipe out Moran and his crew in one fell swoop. Meanwhile, Mafia chief Patsy Lolordo (Guarini) is murdered by Moran's gang with help from one of Capone's own men, Aiello (D'Arcy), who plans to usurp his rule. Incensed, Capone kills Aiello himself before leaving for Florida while McGurn carries out his plan. On Valentine's Day, four of Capone's men storm into Moran's north-side garage dressed as police and open fire,

◀

Ostensibly accurate in its depiction of the events, the movie is a synthesis of historical fact and pure fiction.

killing seven of Moran's outfit in a violent and climactic scene. The bigger budget allows Corman to assemble unrestrained sets, full of period detail, then destroy them with the gangs' unrelenting tommy guns. This destruction is at its most spectacular when Capone comes under fire as he dines in a luxury restaurant; while Capone escapes unscathed, the plush dining room is reduced to rubble. When Moran's boys shake

> ## "YOU MUST BE NEW TO THIS TOWN, MISTER. ONLY AL CAPONE KILLS LIKE THAT." *BUGS MORAN*

down the owner of a small speakeasy, forcing him to sell their own beer, the film offers insight into the business of Prohibition-era rackets. The scene is also a direct quotation from the 1931 film *The Public Enemy*, to which further reference is made when Bugs rubs a lettuce sandwich in his mistress's face, mimicking James Cagney's assault on Mae Clarke with a cut grapefruit.

Its cool detachment from the story makes *The St. Valentine's Day Massacre* very different from later gangster films about the same characters, such as Brian De Palma's *The Untouchables* (1987). Robards makes for a Capone less convincingly Italian, but menacing nonetheless. Despite its success, as a Corman film, *The St. Valentine's Day Massacre* lacks the flourishes of excess evident in his independently produced movies. Unhappy with 20th Century Fox's stricter framework, Corman soon returned to independently produced, lower-budgeted projects. **AK**

► **Al Capone (Robards) amongst the carnage. Fox vetoed the original casting of Orson Welles as Capone, fearing that he was "undirectable."**

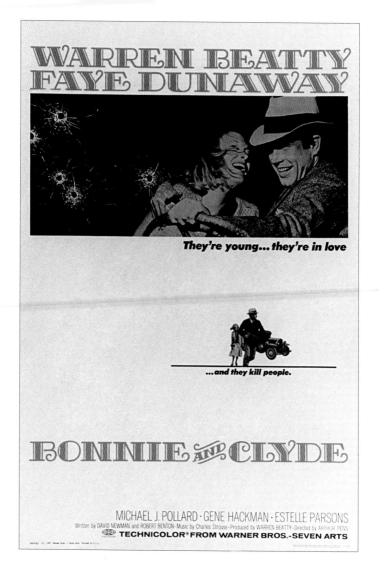

BONNIE AND CLYDE 1967 (U.S.)

Director Arthur Penn **Producer** Warren Beatty **Screenplay** David Newman, Robert Benton **Cinematography** Burnett Guffey **Music** Charles Strouse
Cast Warren Beatty, Faye Dunaway, Gene Hackman, Estelle Parsons, Michael J. Pollard, Denver Pyle, Dub Taylor, Evans Evans, Gene Wilder, Martha Adcock

Despite critics like Bosley Crowther decrying the film, *Bonnie and Clyde* ushered in a new generation of American filmmaking. Although changes to the Production Code made extreme violence more accessible in American cinema, the film was the first to really push those limits in a mainstream Hollywood studio picture.

Clyde Barrow (Beatty) and Bonnie Parker (Dunaway) rob banks throughout the Texas-Oklahoma-Arkansas region in the 1930s as the leaders of the Barrow Gang. *Bonnie and Clyde*, although ostensibly a highly romanticized biopic of the gangsters, also depicts these robbers and killers as Depression-era folk heroes. The two are joined in the Barrow Gang by a mechanic, C. W. Moss (Pollard) and eventually by Clyde's brother, Buck (Hackman), and Buck's wife, Blanche (Parsons).

Despite the wonderful period reconstruction of the era by Burnett Guffey and the Oscar-winning music by Charles Strouse, what really captured American audiences during the "summer of love" was how these notorious outlaws were actually sticking up for the common people hit hard by the Depression. Before we actually see them rob any banks, they

◄
The studio had so little faith in the movie that they offered Beatty 40 percent of the gross rather than a minimal fee. Within six years the film took $70 million worldwide.

break into a seemingly abandoned farmhouse to ransack it. As they emerge, they see the former owners leaving the property, a poor farmer and his family who have been evicted by the banks. Clyde gives the farmer use of his revolver to take some potshots at the "bank's" house, which the farmer readily does. Later in the film, as the Barrow Gang are robbing one of these banks, Clyde asks an old-timer if the money in front of

"THIS HERE'S MISS BONNIE PARKER. I'M CLYDE BARROW. WE ROB BANKS."

CLYDE BARROW

him is his or the bank's. When the old-timer says that it is his own, Clyde tells the man to keep his money; Clyde was interested only in the bank's money. Bonnie and Clyde are portrayed then as radical youths, fighting for America's disenfranchised against the bigger criminals—the banks and the government.

Half comic fairy tale, half brutal fact, *Bonnie and Clyde* reflects the essential ambiguity of its heroes by treading a no-man's-land suspended between reality and fantasy. The weird landscape of derelict towns and verdant highways is stunningly shot by Burnett Guffey in muted tones of green and gold, imbuing a quality of folk legend.

Nominated for 14 Academy Awards in 1968, *Bonnie and Clyde* won two: Estelle Parsons for Best Supporting Actress and Burnett Guffey for Cinematography. **MK**

▶
Faye Dunaway and Warren Beatty work perfectly together as Bonnie and Clyde in a film that was to set a trend for extreme violence on the cinema screen.

There are
two kinds
of people in his
up-tight world:
his victims
and his women.
And sometimes
you can't tell
them apart.

Metro-Goldwyn-Mayer presents
A Judd Bernard-Irwin Winkler
Production

LEE MARVIN
"POINT BLANK"

co-staring
ANGIE DICKINSON KEENAN WYNN · CARROLL O'CONNOR · LLOYD BOCHNER · MICHAEL STRONG
Screenplay by Alexander Jacobs and David Newhouse & Rabe Newhouse Based on the Novel "The Hunter" by Richard Stark
Directed by John Boorman Produced by Judd Bernard and Robert Chartoff
In Panavision® and Metrocolor MGM

POINT BLANK 1967 (U.S.)

Director John Boorman **Producers** Judd Bernard, Robert Chartoff
Screenplay Alexander Jacobs, David Newhouse, Rafe Newhouse (based on a novel
by Donald E. Westlake) **Cinematography** Philip H. Lathrop **Music** Johnny Mandel
Cast Lee Marvin, Sharon Acker, John Vernon, Angie Dickenson, Lloyd Bochner

One of the earliest adaptations of the crime novels of Donald
E. Westlake (written under the pseudonym of Richard Stark),
Point Blank explodes off the screen with a series of violent
slaps, kicks, and punches that helped usher in the neo-noir
film movement in America.

Reeling from a heist double-cross that left him presumed
dead, career criminal Walker (Marvin) sets out to recoup the
$93,000 he is owed from his wife, Lynne (Acker), and pal Mal
Reese (Vernon). With the help of Chris (Dickenson), his wife's
sister, and the mysterious Yost (Keenan Wynn), Walker turns
into a revenge-fueled hurricane that destroys everything in
its path. Walker feels that each subsequent revenge killing
raises his death debt up the ranks of The Organization, a large
criminal enterprize run by Carter (Lloyd Bochner) and Brewster
(Carroll O'Connor).

As a crime film, *Point Blank* brings the moral ambiguity,
femmes fatales, and tough gangsters of film noir to bright,
modern-day California. Marvin, building on the work displayed
in *The Killers* (1964), is as tough and tall as the concrete slabs that
Boorman's camera focuses on all over L.A. and in San Francisco's

◀

**John Boorman
brought the
European
influences
of Resnais
and Godard to
modern California.**

Alcatraz prison. With this film, Marvin seemingly creates the prototype of the stoic, antihero tough guy who hits first and asks questions later, a subgenre that exploded with full force in the 1970s. Director Boorman directs with a sense of urgency, best showcased in an early scene where Marvin bolts down a long corridor while his footsteps echo on the soundtrack. His rhythm and use of elliptical editing skillfully uncovers the links—

"YOU'RE A VERY BAD MAN, WALKER. A VERY DESTRUCTIVE MAN!"

BREWSTER

both personal and professional—between the characters in a series of flashbacks that deconstruct the weeks leading up to the heist. Boorman often creates surreal, dreamlike scenes that unfold on-screen as past and present collide. Interestingly, Boorman has intimated in interviews that the entire film could be merely Walker's death dream as he lies dying.

Point Blank cleverly comments on the changing criminal landscape as brawn tackles brains. Walker's upfront, single-minded revenge is archaic to the modern gangsters and—as crime boss Brewster explains—The Organization is run more like a successful corporation where bosses let grudges be settled from the distance of a hired gun's rifle scope. The picture offers the timeless scenario of man fighting against the system, albeit a criminal one, so much so that it was subsequently remade as *Payback* in 1999, with Mel Gibson. **WW**

▶ **Bullet-headed anachronism Walker (Marvin) keeps wife, Lynne (Acker), quiet while he becomes increasingly puzzled and frustrated.**

BULLITT 1968 (U.S.)

Director Peter Yates **Producer** Philip D'Antoni **Screenplay** Alan Trustman, Harry Kleiner (from the novel *Mute Witness* by Robert L. Pike) **Cinematography** William A. Fraker **Music** Lalo Schifrin **Cast** Steve McQueen, Jacqueline Bisset, Robert Vaughn, Don Gordon, John Aprea, Robert Duvall, Simon Oakland, Norman Fell, Justin Tarr

Bullitt is usually remembered for two things. One is the car chase that spawned a mutitude of imitations. It is certainly an impressive chase sequence shot in real locations, all the more so for being so pared down. There are no major stunts on show here, just skillful high-speed driving through the streets of San Francisco and out into the surrounding countryside. The second memorable thing about the film is its star, Steve McQueen. It has become something of a cliché to say that this coolest of movie actors is at his most cool in *Bullitt*, but it is no less true for that. As the taciturn cop Frank Bullitt, McQueen is mesmerizing in a role that, on paper at least, seems to offer little scope for an actor.

Like its car chase, the film's narrative is pared down. Bullitt is assigned by an ambitious politician (played with convincing slime by Robert Vaughn) to protect a Mobster-turned-state-witness. The Mobster is apparently killed, and Bullitt spends the rest of the movie unraveling a conspiracy that, it turns out, has been created by the Mobster himself, who is still alive and seeking to get away with money he has stolen from what the film refers to as The Organization. Other than the car chase

◄

This cop thriller is elevated to greatness by its remarkable sense of place and its iconic car chase.

and a climactic chase and shoot-out at the airport, there is little action . . . and not a huge amount of detection either. Instead we have scene after scene of Bullitt with witnesses, with his fellow cops, with his accommodating girlfriend (Jacqueline Bissett)—and still we manage to learn remarkably little about this enigmatic man. His girlfriend accuses him with some justification of being emotionally detached, but his

"YOU WORK YOUR SIDE OF THE STREET AND I'LL WORK MINE."

LT. FRANK BULLITT

response is, unsurprisingly, emotionally detached; one gains no clear sense at the end of where this particular relationship is heading and how this man works.

The picture itself also exhibits what might be described as a detached cool style, helped immeasurably in this by Lalo Schifrin's jazz-based score. Indeed the film as a whole can be seen as possessing a jazz-like quality as it improvises around the theme of the solitary cop without ever committing that character to emotional crisis or change. Bullitt's coolness turns out to be as much the product of stasis as it does style. The restraint is typified by the fact that Bullitt uses his pistol only once throughout the film, and then only to fire two shots during the final scenes. For a much more troubled and intense rendition of the lone cop in San Francisco, see Clint Eastwood a few years later in *Dirty Harry* (1971). **PH**

► Steve McQueen as Frank Bullitt in what was arguably his best role.

THE BROTHERHOOD 1968 (U.S.)

Director Martin Ritt **Producer** Kirk Douglas **Screenplay** Lewis John Carlino
Cinematography Frank Bracht, Boris Kaufman **Music** Lalo Schifrin **Cast** Kirk
Douglas, Alex Cord, Irene Papas, Luther Adler, Susan Strasberg, Murray Hamilton,
Eduardo Cianelli, Joe De Santis, Connie Scott, Val Avery, Val Bisoglio, Alan Hewitt

Released at the tail end of the 1960s and featuring screen
legend Kirk Douglas as Frank Ginetta, an aging Mafia henchman
stubbornly railing against the syndication and legitimization of
his beloved Mob, *The Brotherhood* should have been a hit.
However, the picture was greeted with an almost universal
critical panning and audience indifference upon its initial
release. Perversely, Francis Ford Coppola's 1972 epic *The
Godfather*, which shares numerous aspects of its plot with that
of *The Brotherhood*—albeit focusing on a different era in Mafia
folklore—was released no more than four years later and
became instantly recognized as a classic.

Kirk Douglas' Ginetta is a man clearly steeped in traditions and
loyal to those codes of masculinity and kinship bestowed
upon him by his experiences in the Mob. Unfortunately his
younger brother Victor (Cord) returns from the Vietnam War
and, eager for their operation to diversify and align with an
international crime syndicate, betrays the very codes that
Frank holds so dear. After Frank ruthlessly murders Victor's
father-in-law and Mob boss Dominic Bertolo (Adler) in revenge
for his father's own killing years earlier, he hides out in Sicily

◄

**A flop at the box
office, this movie
nearly persuaded
Paramount not
to make *The
Godfather*.**

with other members of the old guard. The idyllic quiet of small-town Sicily seems to suit Frank, until Victor is persuaded by the syndicate he so faithfully courts to avenge Bertolo's killing. He arrives to a less than warm reception from Frank and the sycophantic old Mafia warhorses he has surrounded himself with. *The Brotherhood* depicts the inhabitants of the murky world of underground, organized crime as an ethnically mixed

"A BLUNT, SQUARE AND SENTIMENTAL MAFIA MOVIE WHOSE HEART BELONGS TO THE SENIOR SOLDIERS." VINCENT CANBY

bag of crooks keen to unite and exploit each other's strengths if it means getting paid. The conflict at the heart of the picture is that of the aforementioned crooks and the crumbling old guard of Mafiosos, out of touch with the fast-paced modern world and resistant to its seemingly endless opportunities—but still vicious enough to do it some final damage.

Lewis John Carlino's screenplay is steeped in twisted Mob nostalgia, yet it pulls no punches in showing the brutality that resides at the core of such organizations, and it is an impressively contemporary account of 1960s organized crime. The initially harsh judgments passed on *The Brotherhood* do not do director Martin Ritt any justice, and very welcome reevaluations by modern critics have appeared in recent years, acknowledging the film's quality and allowing it to emerge from the large, domineering shadow cast by *The Godfather*. **MW**

►
A pensive Frank Ginetta, played by Kirk Douglas.

BLOODY MAMA 1970 (U.S.)

Director Roger Corman **Producer** Roger Corman **Screenplay** Don Peters, Robert Thom **Cinematography** John Alonzo **Music** Don Randi **Cast** Shelley Winters, Pat Hingle, Don Stroud, Diane Varsi, Bruce Dern, Clint Kimbrough, Robert De Niro, Robert Walden, Alex Nicol, Pamela Dunlap, Michael Fox, Scatman Crothers

Roger Corman's further contribution to exploitation pictures coheres in *Bloody Mama* with his other films for AIP, addressing a youthful audience with the theme of adolescent rebellion, with occasional nudity and a sexually charged narrative.

Corman asserts his intention to tell the "true" story of Kate "Ma" Barker and her gangster sons in a humorous inversion of the usual disclaimer. We are carried back to the Depression era and the rare invasion by a woman of a traditionally male-dominated territory: not the urban space of mean streets, but a pretty pastoral world, populated by hoedowns, remote cottages, alligators, and assorted backwoods characters. *Bloody Mama* frustrates viewers expecting a pacy gangster film—its excessive nature lies in its Oedipal plot and sexual innuendo.

Initially a young Kate (Winters) runs through a sunlit woodland, pursued and captured by her brothers for her pa's enjoyment. Weeping, she declares that she will "get her some sons." With the Oedipal agenda in motion, but subject to no further social exploration of the psychology of this woman from the Ozarks, we cut to the rural household of would-be domestic goddess Kate. Aware that her emasculated husband and adolescent sons

◀ **Corman's foray into rural gangsterdom makes no bones about its antisocial antiheroes—the Barker clan are blatant public enemies.**

are merely instruments of her ambition and sexual pleasure, a jealous Kate has them testify to the sheriff to the superiority of her pies, packs their bags, and assures her tearful husband that she will be found in a "palace," or not at all. Thus driven into aimless flight by a desire for riches, she will "do anything" for her sons and they for her, including kidnapping and murder. Their destiny is suicide, the Oedipal family collapsing in on itself.

"FAMILIES WHO SLAY TOGETHER STAY TOGETHER . . . IN A SEPULCHRE MADE FOR TWO?" PROMOTIONAL POSTER

Is it a step too far to align this film with feminism? There are brief inserts of documentary material that offer a broader context for Ma's exploits, guided by Kate's voice-over. She discusses the changes women have experienced—they wear revealing clothes and smoke in public! She rejoices that she never had girls and justifies direct action in relation to the poverty of the Depression.

Seen as a response to "women's issues," this is not the only film to investigate matriarchal family life and its ensuing disorder in this period. However, the real interest of *Bloody Mama* lies in its unraveling of the Oedipal narrative, its multiplication of father figures and unmasking of the monstrous mother, rather than in its spotlight on social issues through the gangster genre, though it does glance at rural life in the South and its rise to prominence in the figure of murdering Ma Barker. **VC**

► Shelley Winters as Ma Barker, the legendary matriarch.

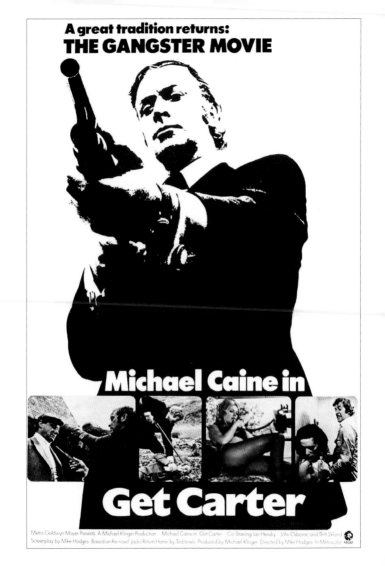

GET CARTER 1971 (U.K.)

Director Mike Hodges **Producer** Michael Klinger **Screenplay** Mike Hodges
(based on Ted Lewis's novel *Jack's Return Home*) **Cinematography** Wolfgang
Suschitzky **Music** Roy Budd **Cast** Michael Caine, Ian Hendry, Britt Ekland,
John Osborne, Petra Markham, Tony Beckley, Geraldine Moffat, George Sewell

1971 was a seminal year for the gritty crime genre with classic films such as *Dirty Harry* and *The French Connection* being released. Beating them to the punch in the early part of the year was the U.K. export *Get Carter*, a brutal revenge thriller that proves family above all else trumps the gangster code of ethics.

London-based gangster Jack Carter (Caine) returns to his hometown of Newcastle-upon-Tyne to attend the funeral of his brother Frank. Unsatisfied with the official cause of death, Carter begins his own investigation, which raises the ire of the local hoodlums. Carter's exploration leads him to shady businessmen, crime bosses, and loose women. Proving his criminal intuition correct, Carter discovers that his brother was killed over a stag film featuring Doreen (Markham), Jack's niece, who may or may not be his biological daughter.

Based on the novel *Jack's Return Home*, Mike Hodges made his theatrical debut with this pioneering film that exposes the seedy underbelly of English crime that subsists inside bars, betting parlors, strip clubs, and pool halls. Alive with fervid industrialism, Newcastle is shown as a city of dilapidated row houses, ostensibly choking on the smog from the factories

◄

As well as creating the screenplay, this was Hodges' first film as a director. It was shot in just 40 days on location in northeast England. Roy Bud's jazzy soundtrack keeps it real too.

that dot the landscape. The film's nihilism factor is high within these working-class confines and, appropriately, culminates with Carter chasing his brother's killer into a gloomy coal-dumping facility. Surprising moments of black comedy do lighten the film's tone on occasion, including a phone sex conversation Carter has in front of his landlady and a naked Carter escorting some thugs outside with a shotgun. But the

> ## "COME ON, JACK, PUT IT AWAY. YOU KNOW YOU'RE NOT GOING TO USE IT."
>
> *CON MCCARTY*

fisticuffs are the film's highlight as Caine punches, kicks, and humiliates anyone in his way. All of the revenge is driven on-screen by Roy Budd's thumping score, a piece that set new standards for musical scores.

Caine, heretofore a charmer even in villainous roles, is a revelation as the grim Carter. With his clipped speech and unwavering, dead stare, Caine personifies the no-nonsense English organized crime enforcer, and Carter became an iconic figure. Unlike its American counterparts, however, *Get Carter*'s unseemly display of realistic violence was frowned upon during its initial release. The subsequent years have allowed time to catch up with the film's reputation, however, and *Get Carter* is now considered a groundbreaking classic of the revenge genre. Hollywood produced a remake in 2000, with Sylvester Stallone as Jack Carter and Caine in a supporting role. **WW**

► Caine as Carter in the movie that *Total Film* magazine named the greatest British film of all time in 2004.

SHAFT 1971 (U.S.)

Director Gordon Parks **Producer** Joel Freeman **Screenplay** Ernest Tidyman, John D. F. Black (based on the novel by Ernest Tidyman) **Cinematography** Urs Furrer **Music** Isaac Hayes, J. J. Johnson **Cast** Richard Roundtree, Moses Gunn, Charles Cioffi, Christopher St. John, Gwenn Mitchell, Lawrence Pressman

On the heels of *They Call Me MISTER Tibbs!* (1970), *Cotton Comes to Harlem* (1970), and *Sweet Sweetback's Baadasssss Song* (1971), Gordon Parks' *Shaft* proved to be one of the most culturally significant films of the decade.

Private detective John Shaft (Roundtree) is hired by Harlem crime boss Bumpy Jonas (Gunn) to find his kidnapped daughter. Bumpy suspects a militant African American group led by Ben Buford (St. John) is behind the kidnapping, but Shaft's detective work quickly uncovers a more sinister plan. With the help of Lt. Vic Androzzi (Cioffi), Shaft exposes a race war simmering between the Italian Mafia and Jonas.

Primarily known for its entertainment value, *Shaft* is also significant in terms of both the character and its portrayal of race relations on-screen. With Shaft generally considered the first black action hero, the importance of African American audiences seeing such a successful figure standing up to "the man" just seven years after the Civil Rights Act of 1964 cannot be underestimated. As wisecracking and smooth as Philip Marlowe, Shaft stood toe-to-toe and matched swear-for-swear against his white male adversaries. The relationship between

◄
The film is based on a work by Ernest Tidyman, who was an editor at *The New York Times*. He sold the *Shaft* movie rights to M.G.M. before it was published in 1970.

Shaft and Lt. Androzzi shows a great rapport as the two men help each other as easily as they trade racial barbs, an extension of the earlier Sidney Poitier–Rod Steiger relationship from *In the Heat of the Night* (1967). Accordingly, *Shaft*—a modestly-budgeted studio film—was one of the highest-grossing films of the year and solidified the Blaxploitation film movement in America. The film is significant in also helping to further

"I GOT TO FEELING LIKE A MACHINE, AND THAT'S NO WAY TO FEEL."

JOHN SHAFT

establish Gordon Parks as the first successful mainstream African American film director. A celebrated photo-journalist and documentarian, Parks offers a version of New York City rarely seen by audiences to this point, and his work here helped pave the way for subsequent African American directors. Equally successful was the film's soundtrack by Isaac Hayes, which spent more than a year on the music charts and won three Grammys. The "Theme from *Shaft*" also won the Academy Award for Best Original Song, making Hayes the first African American composer to win this award. Former male model Richard Roundtree also launched a prolific career off the picture. He reprised the John Shaft role in two sequels (*Shaft's Big Score* [1972], *Shaft in Africa* [1973]), a short-lived TV series, and nearly thirty years later in *Shaft* (2000), featuring Samuel L. Jackson as Shaft's nephew who shares the same name. **WW**

►
Richard Roundtree as Shaft, the epitome of 1970s style.

THE FRENCH CONNECTION 1971 (U.S.)

Director William Friedkin **Producer** Philip D'Antoni **Screenplay** Ernest Tidyman (from the novel by Robin Moore) **Cinematography** Owen Roizman **Music** Don Ellis **Cast** Gene Hackman, Roy Scheider, Fernando Rey, Tony Lo Bianco, Marcel Bozzuffi, Frédéric de Pasquale, Bill Hickman, Ann Rebbot, Harold Gary, Arlene Farber

The French Connection seems like an odd movie to have won the Best Picture Oscar in 1971; it is not exactly the kind of film to be recognized by the Academy for excellence, despite the remarkable performance by Gene Hackman (legendary New York City newspaper columnist Jimmy Breslin was originally hired to play Hackman's role, even completing three weeks of rehearsals with co-star Roy Scheider before William Friedkin decided to recast him). And of course, it features the single-greatest car chase sequence of any American movie to date.

The French Connection tells the true(ish) story of how a hard-working, equitably racist cop, Jimmy "Popeye" Doyle (Hackman), and his partner Buddy Russo (Scheider) broke up an international heroin ring trying to import more than 60 kilograms of pure-grade smack into the United States, until that point the largest drug bust in American police history.

What is particularly remarkable about the film is its juxtaposition between the wealth of the European drug lords and the poverty of the hardworking New York police officers. The mise-en-scène reflects this juxtaposition too. The European sequences are filmed in high-key color, with a certain 1970s

◄

The movie established the careers of both Friedkin and Hackman, and was instrumental in ushering in an era of neo-realist directors during the early 1970s.

European quality to them, much like many of the Italian-produced police films ubiquitous during that period. On the other hand, the New York sequences are almost always filmed using a handheld camera, with gray and washed-out cinematography, anticipating the gritty urban reality of the Blaxploitation movies that emerged the same year (the film's screenwriter, Ernest Tidyman, wrote the novel *Shaft* in 1970).

"ALL RIGHT, POPEYE'S HERE! GET YOUR HANDS ON YOUR HEADS!"

JIMMY "POPEYE" DOYLE

And oh, that car chase. Friedkin has said this scene was shot entirely out of sequence, over a period of five weeks; amazingly, it did not involve any solid day-to-day shooting. Regardless, the chase was widely considered the best-ever put on film at the time, overtaking *Bullitt* (1968) for that honor. Friedkin later tried (and failed) to outdo himself with a chase sequence in *To Live and Die in L.A.* (1985).

At the heart of *The French Connection* is perhaps the most complex police detective in Hollywood history. Doyle isn't a corrupt cop; that would be too simplistic. He's simply flawed. Friedkin and Hackman create empathy for the character, but never sympathy. We are not invited to condone Doyle's racist remarks, and the film treats its audience with enough intelligence to understand that this character is, at heart, an asshole. Popeye himself seems to know this too. **MK**

► Gene Hackman gave a truly exceptional performance as Popeye.

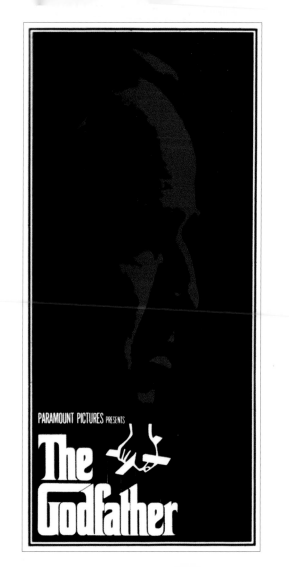

THE GODFATHER 1972 (U.S.)

Director Francis Ford Coppola **Producer** Albert S. Ruddy **Screenplay** Mario Puzo, Francis Ford Coppola (from the novel by Mario Puzo) **Cinematography** Gordon Willis **Music** Nino Rota **Cast** Marlon Brando, Al Pacino, James Caan, John Cazale, Diane Keaton, Robert Duvall, Talia Shire, Richard Castellano, Sterling Hayden

No gangster movie is more synonymous with the genre than *The Godfather*, which swept the Oscars in '72 and revitalized the genre for the next 35 years. Endlessly quoted and referred to throughout popular culture, the film remains an excellent piece of American pulp cinema buoyed up by some utterly remarkable performances: not just the Oscar-winning turn by Marlon Brando and the career-making one by Al Pacino, but the exceptionally strong supporting roles by James Caan, John Cazale, Robert Duvall, and Diane Keaton.

The Godfather tells the story of the Corleone family in the immediate post-war years, the period where the United States emerges as a superpower, and this national development is reflected in microcosm through the Corleones. The youngest of the Corleone sons, Michael (Pacino), returns home to New York after serving in the army during World War II with his WASPish schoolteacher girlfriend Kay (Keaton). Throughout his life, this favored son has resisted the draws of the family's crime businesses and is slated to be the first Corleone to be a legitimate success. But fate keeps intervening, always drawing Michael deeper into the underworld until eventually, with his hot-headed brother

◄
Coppola was not Paramount's first choice to direct— Sergio Leone declined the job in order to work on his own gangster opus *Once Upon A Time In America*.

Sonny (Caan) gunned down and his father largely retired, this reluctant mobster takes over the family business. Coppola always saw *The Godfather* not as a gangster film, but as a film that accurately depicted the kind of Italian-American family he grew up in; he wanted to capture the authenticity of his cultural experience. The film's tagline, "The saga of an American family," reflects this desire to minimize the mob focus and emphasize the

"A MAN THAT DOESN'T SPEND TIME WITH HIS FAMILY CAN NEVER BE A REAL MAN." *DON VITO CORLEONE*

centrality of the ethnic family. In fact, the word "Mafia" is never spoken once in the entire picture, although rumor has it that this was an attempt at keeping Italian-American lobby groups from interfering with filming.

One of the most remarkable things about *The Godfather*, beyond the performances, is Gordon Willis' cinematography, an interior chiaroscuro lighting pattern that makes every shadow menacing. His constant interplay between light and dark evokes the dark motives behind every private conversation and meeting. His exterior photography, conversely, is always high key, reflecting the openness and honesty of the Corleone family's public face. The only exception to this lighting schema are the Sicilian sequences; once Michael is out of New York and away from the family, there is no need for the same duplicity he knew in the city, and so the cinematography is consistently high key. **MK**

▶

The Godfather, Don Vito Corleone, played by Marlon Brando with padded cheeks. He won, but refused to accept, an Academy Award for Best Actor.

DILLINGER 1973 (U.S.)

Director John Milius **Producer** Buzz Feitshans **Screenplay** John Millius
Cinematography Jules Brenner **Music** Barry DeVorzon **Cast** Warren Oates,
Ben Johnson, Michelle Phillips, Cloris Leachman, Harry Dean Stanton, Geoffrey Lewis,
John P. Ryan, Richard Dreyfuss, Steve Kanaly, John Martino, Roy Jenson, Read Morgan

Dillinger is more than just an excellent biopic of a notorious
gangster. It is the definitive version of the Dillinger story in spite,
or because, of its "freedom" in dealing with the facts. It is graced
by the impeccable Warren Oates as the larger-than-life man
who robbed banks for a living. Paired with the equally excellent
Ben Johnson as his arch-nemesis, the dedicated G-Man Purvis
of the FBI, Oates breathes life into the archetypal robber.

John Milius wisely chooses to present this story as a mythical
battle, with both main characters sketched through clever
vignettes: Dillinger is a gentleman–robber, a folk hero, a
superstar relishing the attention of the media and audience (his
"victims") even more than the money. This doesn't mean that
he is glamorized: more than once you can see the cruelty of his
ways and vivid collateral damage of his exploits. The same goes
for his opponent: Purvis is a fearless hero, erect in the face of
danger, gallant toward the ladies, and strangely respectful
toward his enemy, but also not exceedingly law-abiding himself
("Shoot Dillinger and we'll figure out a way to make it legal," he
says at one point). While the background of this story is obvious
(the Great Depression of the 1930s), it is kept where it should

◄

In this movie, John
Milius indirectly
pays homage to
all the different
media that have
contributed to the
Dillinger legend.

be—in the background. Milius never strives to over-explain his characters, who remain balanced between history and legend. The script is written with an admirable economy, managing not only to cover the basic events in Dillinger's career but also find the time for some special treasures, like the episode with the stubborn, fearless geezer at the gas pump, or a priceless moment when Purvis shows his gun to a boy who would rather

"I ROB BANKS FOR A LIVING, WHAT DO YOU DO?"

JOHN DILLINGER

grow up to be a gangster. A typical example of an invented but so-good-it-must-be-true moment is the scene in which Purvis spots Dillinger in a restaurant where he's celebrating with his fiancée. Instead of grabbing his gun or calling for backup, he sends the gangster and his lady a bottle of champagne, promising that their next encounter won't be so gentle. It is moments like these, together with the relentlessly bloody shoot-out scenes and countless memorable, witty pieces of dialogue, that raise this film far above a standard gangster melodrama and make it a unique, clever, layered, and enjoyable piece of Americana.

While paying homage to the collective interpretations of the Dillinger legend, Milius, who like his contemporary "movie brat" directors had a passion for classic Hollywood films, keeps things the right side of nostalgia throughout the movie. **DO**

▶
Because of his daring exploits, the real-life John Dillinger (played here by Warren Oates) became America's own folk-hero during the Great Depression.

MEAN STREETS

"Exquisite, savage,
compassionate and brilliant."
—Joseph Gelmis, Newsday

WARNER BROS. A Warner Communications Company presents A TAPLIN-PERRY-SCORSESE
Production "MEAN STREETS" A MARTIN SCORSESE movie Starring ROBERT DE NIRO and HARVEY KEITEL.
David Proval, Amy Robinson, Richard Romanus, with Cesare Danova as "Giovanni".
Executive Producer E. LEE PERRY Screenplay by MARTIN SCORSESE and MARDIK MARTIN
Produced by JONATHAN T. TAPLIN · Directed by MARTIN SCORSESE Technicolor®

Celebrating Warner Bros. 50th Anniversary
A Warner Communications Company
R RESTRICTED

MEAN STREETS 1973 (U.S.)

Director Martin Scorsese **Producer** Jonathan T. Taplin **Screenplay** Martin Scorsese, Mardik Martin **Cinematography** Kent Wakeford **Cast** Harvey Keitel, Robert De Niro, David Proval, Amy Robinson, Richard Romanus, Cesare Danova, Victor Argo, George Memmoli, Lenny Scaletta, Jeannie Bell, Murray Mosten

Although not the directorial debut of Martin Scorsese, *Mean Streets* was the first film that really shows the imprinteur of the emerging auteur. It was also the first collaboration between Scorsese and Robert De Niro, the actor who would become synonymous with the director's films.

Mean Streets tells the story of four friends from New York's Little Italy: Charlie (Keitel), Tony (Proval), Michael (Romanus) and Johnny Boy (De Niro). Charlie is an up-and-coming mobster working for his uncle Tony, who owns the bar the four friends hang out at, and Johnny Boy is the weak one of the pack, perpetually in debt to the others. Charlie is also having a surreptitious affair with Johnny Boy's cousin, Teresa (Robinson), an epileptic who the community does not think is a suitable woman for Charlie because of her condition.

Emerging in 1973, between the two *Godfather* films, *Mean Streets* reflects the semi-autobiographical world of small-time hoodlums and players. Although the movie is rough and raw, primarily because it was being filmed non-union and under the radar of the Teamsters, it does reflect both the director's signature style of dialogue and explosive violence. The movie is

◄

This is the movie that forged the Scorsese and De Niro partnership.

primarily noteworthy for its soundtrack; this was one of the first pictures, along with *American Graffiti* (1973), to not use a composed soundtrack, and instead use popular music throughout (rumored to be entirely from Scorsese's own collection).

Looking back at *Mean Streets* now, the influence of the French New Wave is notable: Scorsese jump-cuts throughout scenes much like *Breathless* (1960), and often uses a handheld

"I F*CK YOU RIGHT WHERE YOU BREATHE BECAUSE I DON'T GIVE TWO SH*TS ABOUT YOU OR NOBODY ELSE." *JOHNNY BOY*

camera to give immediacy to the action. At one point, the four friends decide to go off to the movies, a moment in the film that offers no narrative significance beyond further establishing their characters as those weaned on classical Hollywood cinema—it's a moment that could have come right out of a Truffaut film.

Mean Streets is the closest American cinema has seen to developing a new wave of its own—slightly derivative of its French counterpart, but wholly a slice of personalized and authentic American culture.

▶

Robert De Niro is memorable as Johnny Boy in this gritty take on New York life. The role was the starting point of De Niro's rise to fame.

Scorsese's energetic, insightful direction gives vigor to the performances and infuses the sharp dialogue, violent action, and authentic hustle of New York with vitality. *Mean Streets* is a landmark movie of the '70s, and secured a National Society of Film Critics award for Best Supporting Actor for De Niro. **MK**

THIEVES LIKE US 1974 (U.S.)

Director Robert Altman **Producer** Jerry Bick **Screenplay** Calder Willingham, Joan Tewkesbury, Robert Altman, based on a novel by Edward Anderson **Cinematography** Jean Boffety **Cast** Keith Carradine, Shelley Duvall, John Schuck, Bert Remsen, Louise Fletcher, Ann Latham, Tom Skerritt, Al Scott, John Roper

Thieves Like Us is derived from Edward Anderson's 1937 novel of the same title, which Nicholas Ray previously adapted for the screen as *They Live by Night* (1948). Altman's version closely follows the book to tell the story of three escaped convicts—T-Dub (Remsen), Chicamaw (Schuck), and the youthful Bowie (Carradine)—who take refuge with relatives, all while carrying out a number of bank robberies in Depression-era Mississippi. They first stay with Dee Mobley (Skerritt) and his shy daughter Keechie (Duvall), and later with T-Dub's steely sister-in-law, Mattie (Fletcher). When injured in a car accident Bowie is cared for by Keechie, the two "innocents" gradually falling in love and later moving to set up temporary house at a lakeside cabin. Despite Keechie's pleas, Bowie rejoins his gangster companions for another bank job, but in the aftermath T-Dub is killed and Chicamaw captured. Bowie returns to Keechie, who has realized she is pregnant, and the couple move to a motel. Ultimately, Bowie is betrayed by Mattie, and Keechie looks on in anguish as he is gunned down by police. In a departure from the novel (where the lovers die together), *Thieves Like Us* ends with Keechie (and unborn child) leaving to begin a new life.

◀

Robert Altman was able to reinterpret Edward Anderson's novel by shooting on location in Mississippi, using local residents as extras.

Like other Altman films of the 1970s—notably, *McCabe & Mrs. Miller* (1971) and *The Long Goodbye* (1973)—*Thieves Like Us* is a revisionist genre movie, a gangster film that comments upon (and de-romanticizes) predecessors such as *They Live by Night* and *Bonnie and Clyde* (1967). More broadly, *Thieves Like Us* is a de-mythologizing account of free-enterprise America, one that contemplates the development of media communications and

"WE WERE REALLY TRYING TO GET THE AUDIENCE TO THINK ABOUT THE ATMOSPHERE OF CRIME." ROBERT ALTMAN

advertising (print, radio), and their ability to influence the "reality" (the character and behavior) of the protagonists. Devoid of a conventional music score, the film employs radio programs and news items of the day to contrast with, and reflect ironically upon, the gangsters' marginally successful robberies and their personal relationships. In a telling sequence, a line from a radio dramatization of *The Tragedy of Romeo & Juliet*—"Thus did Romeo and Juliet consummate their first interview by falling madly in love"—accompanies Bowie and Keechie's first sexual encounter and is repeated a second and third time, as a lightly humorous refrain, as their lovemaking continues. The passage exemplifies the film's ironic romanticism, just as the phrase "thieves like us" indicates that the gangsters are only doing what those in private enterprise accomplish in socially sanctioned ways. **CV**

► Keith Carradine (left) as young Bowie, one of the gang of three who go on a bank-robbing rampage.

THE GODFATHER PART II 1974 (U.S.)

Director Francis Ford Coppola **Producer** Francis Ford Coppola
Screenplay Mario Puzo, Francis Ford Coppola (from the novel by Mario Puzo)
Cinematography Gordon Willis **Music** Nino Rota **Cast** Robert De Niro, Al Pacino, John Cazale, Diane Keaton, Robert Duvall, Bruno Kirby, Lee Strasberg

The Godfather: Part II is possibly the first case where "Part 2" has been used to indicate a motion picture sequel, at least according to Coppola himself. And, as many people have said in the past, this film is one of the few sequels that may be greater than the original; it won more Oscars than the first, and is the only case to date where a sequel has won the Best Picture nod together with five others: Adapted Screenplay, Director, Music, Art Direction, and Supporting Actor (De Niro).

The Godfather: Part II utilizes a complex time frame, occupying two parallel time periods that reflect and comment on each other. In one, Michael Corleone (Pacino) has moved his family to Lake Tahoe and is still attempting to legitimize the Corleone business interests, this time using government connections. In the second story, which comes from the unused sections of Puzo's novel Coppola didn't film for the first *Godfather*, we see young Vito as a boy escaping to America from Sicily and then as a young man (De Niro) beginning his crime empire.

Although there is no denying that *The Godfather: Part II* is at least the equal of the first film—the acting is again uniformly excellent and the stories are utterly compelling—the political

◄

Complex and ambitious, *The Godfather: Part II* with its sequel/ prequel format is considered by many to surpass the first *Godfather*.

machinations of the Corleone family and their business interests in Cuba on the eve of the Revolution make the sequel a more "serious" movie than its predecessor. In fact, *The Godfather Part II* really lays the groundwork for future films that try to scoop as many Oscars as possible. This film has both the "serious political" story *and* the "costume drama" elements. What is most interesting here, though, is the re-creation of "Old New York."

"IF HISTORY HAS TAUGHT US ANYTHING, IT'S THAT YOU CAN KILL ANYONE." MICHAEL CORLEONE

Early on, young Vito and a friend go off to a popular theater to see an Italian immigrant operetta, *Sans sa Mama*—an actual immigrant play from the time, written by Coppola's own grandfather. Although some immigrant films from this period have survived, mostly in Yiddish, with this operetta we see some evidence of the actual Italian immigrant theater performed in New York back in the day.

The Godfather: Part II not only features a very strong early performance by De Niro, but the young Clemenza is played by Bruno Kirby (before becoming Billy Crystal's sidekick), and during the sequences showing the Senate investigation of organized crime, two of the senators are cameos by none other than prolific director Roger Corman and screenwriter Richard Matheson. This is without doubt a masterful sequel, but also an innovative and exceptional movie in its own right. **MK**

► A young Vito Corleone (De Niro) defends his family's pride and safety in 1920s New York.

BUGSY MALONE 1976 (U.K.)

Director Alan Parker **Producer** Alan Marshall **Screenplay** Alan Parker
Cinematography Peter Biziou, Michael Seresin **Music** Paul Williams **Cast** Scott
Baio, Florrie Dugger, Jodie Foster, John Cassisi, Martin Lev, Paul Murphy, Sheridan
Earl Russell, Albin "Humpty" Jenkins, Paul Chirelstein, Andrew Paul, Davidson Knight

The promotional tagline for *Bugsy Malone* read: "There has never
been a movie like it," and more than 30 years after its release,
there still hasn't been. In this G-rated gangster musical based
loosely around stories of real-life mobsters like Al Capone, all the
characters are played by twelve-year-old children. The film tells
the story of smooth operator Bugsy Malone (Baio), who interrupts
dates with his girl Blousey (Dugger) to help top gangster Fat Sam
(Cassisi) escape from a number of close calls. His rule is being
challenged by rival gangster Dandy Dan (Lev), who, in this
Prohibition era, ruins Sam's lucrative sarsaparilla racket and
destroys most of his gang with cream-topped pies and splurge
guns filled with the same deadly custard. With friend Leroy Smith
(Murphy), Bugsy comes up with a plan to destroy Dandy Dan's
gang, and the film climaxes in a riotous food fight/showdown at
Fat Sam's Grand Slam speakeasy. During the chaos, Bugsy
escapes from the scene with Blousey to leave for Hollywood.
Despite the carnage at Fat Sam's, a song by the pianist leaves all
rivalries (and the gangster genre's rules) forgotten when the
entire cast break into a closing song-and-dance number. A
diffused and glossy patina envelopes the scaled-down sets and

◀
**Former advertising
copywriter Alan
Parker made this
(his first feature)
as a children's
film. However,
its subversion
of the gangster
genre gives it a far
broader appeal.**

shrunken scenarios of *Bugsy Malone*, recalling the glamor of classical Hollywood. Director Alan Parker reportedly remarked that this was achieved by holding an imported shade of Christian Dior stocking over the camera lens. As Parker's directorial debut, *Bugsy Malone* is a triumph of pure dedication, and was made with support from the National Film Finance Corporation during the movie industry recession of the 1970s.

> ## *"IT WAS A LABOR OF LOVE BY A LOT OF PEOPLE MAKING THEIR FIRST FILM."* ALAN PARKER

One of the film's most memorable sequences introduces a young Jodie Foster as Fat Sam's moll, Tallulah, on stage in a dress-up box satin gown and pin curls where, surrounded by underage tiny showgirls and backup "singers," she mimes the lyrically suggestive song "My Name Is Tallulah." *Bugsy Malone*'s peculiarity rests partly on these musical numbers, where largely inexperienced child actors lip-synch to a soundtrack recorded entirely by adults. Were their lips moving in time, it wouldn't matter, for both the timbre of the recorded voices (including composer Paul Williams' own) and the songs' compositional sophistication grate against the dress-up party aesthetic. The film revels in this artificiality. Bullets are replaced with custard and the scaled-down cars run on pedal power. The children perform the gangster genre without any sense of its historical significance, and this lends *Bugsy Malone* a curious authenticity. **AK**

► Striking fear into anyone in their way, Dandy Dan's men have their splurge guns at the ready.

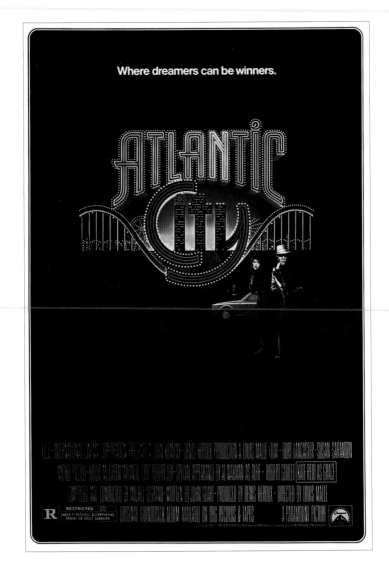

ATLANTIC CITY 1980 (CANADA · FRANCE)

Director Louis Malle **Producers** Denis Héroux, John Kemeny **Screenplay** John Guare **Cinematography** Richard Ciupka **Music** Michel Legrand **Cast** Burt Lancaster, Susan Sarandon, Michel Piccoli, Hollis McLaren, Robert Joy, Moses Znaimer, Robert Goulet, Al Waxman, Kate Reid, Angus MacInnes, Sean Sullivan

Louis Malle's *Atlantic City*, one of the most critically acclaimed motion pictures of the French director's remarkable career, merges setting and character to reveal the "American Dream" as an illusory construction. The gambling Mecca that Malle's camera captures in the film's few-but-crucial exterior shots is an oceanside eyesore undergoing a widespread demolition. Such images prove an appropriate allegory for the various protagonists struggling to survive on society's margins. Indeed, their aspirations and foibles are the real focus of the film's delicately constructed narrative penned by the celebrated playwright John Guare (*House of Blue Leaves*): Lou Pascal (Lancaster), an aging numbers runner reduced to taking nickel-and-dime bets, longs for the financial acumen and high-roller lifestyle that he feels has passed him by; Sally Matthews (Sarandon), a waitress at an oyster bar, desires to move on with her life following the dissolution of her marriage; Grace Pinza (Reid), who moved to Atlantic City forty years earlier with the dream of winning a Betty Grable look-alike contest, clings to a tenuous veil of illusion with the desperation of a modern-day Blanche DuBois. These characters form a poignant bond as their lives and dreams, like

◄
Malle was having difficulty with the original script, until John Guare stepped in and rewrote it, saving the day. It was his idea to set the film in Atlantic City.

the city in which they live, crumble about them. Their lives are upset when Sally's ex-husband, Dave (Joy), and his new wife, Sally's younger sister Chrissie (McLaren), arrive with a cache of drugs stolen from Philadelphia mobsters who soon come looking for their pilfered goods. More a character-driven chamber play than a sprawling epic along the lines of Martin Scorsese's *Casino* (1995), *Atlantic City* captures the central

"YES, IT USED TO BE BEAUTIFUL—WHAT WITH THE RACKETS, WHORING, GUNS."

LOU PASCAL

protagonist's tenderness and pathos. That said, Malle still injects his film with more than enough suspense and violence to satisfy audiences longing for what they have come to expect from a traditional crime drama.

Furthermore, Malle's reliance upon ambient music rather than a conventional score adds to the work's realist tone; music originates from within the scene, often via radios or musical instruments. For example, in one of *Atlantic City*'s earliest and most memorable sequences, Sally returns from work and washes her breasts over the kitchen sink, using lemon juice to eradicate the odor of seafood. Unaware that Lou is watching, she luxuriates in the moment, moving to the classical music playing from a nearby radio. It is such nuances of everyday life as experienced by people longing for a sense of personal fulfillment that makes *Atlantic City* a work of profound compassion. **JM**

► Susan Sarandon puts great characterization into the part of Sally, the waitress whose life takes a dramatic turn when the mobsters come looking for their stolen goods.

THE LONG GOOD FRIDAY 1980 (U.K.)

Director John Mackenzie **Producer** Barry Hanson **Screenplay** Barrie Keeffe
Cinematography Phil Meheux **Music** Francis Monkman **Cast** Bob Hoskins,
Helen Mirren, Dave King, Bryan Marshall, Eddie Constantine, Stephen Davis, Derek
Thompson, Paul Freeman, George Coulouris, Pierce Brosnan, Leo Dolan, Brian Hall

The first image we see of Harold Shand (Hoskins), the gangland
boss of *The Long Good Friday*, is of him walking through Heathrow
Airport to the sound of Francis Monkman's electronic score,
announcing not only the arrival of a major new character in the
annals of British crime cinema, but also the arrival of a new star in
the sheer physical presence of Bob Hoskins. For many, this was the
film that introduced us to the remarkable Hoskins.

Set during Easter weekend, as Shand tries to broker a land deal
with the New York Mafia to buy up the then-derelict London
docklands for a massive redevelopment project, unseen players
are at work trying to bring Shand's empire crashing down. His best
friend is stabbed while at a swimming pool, his mother's chauffeur
is killed by a car bomb meant for her, his prize pub is blown up,
and a third bomb is discovered, unexploded, in another of his
restaurants. Shand, along with his devoted second wife, Victoria
(Mirren), and trusted lieutenant Jeff (Thompson), try to find out
who is having a go at him while trying to save face in front of his
American counterparts without jeopardizing his real-estate deal.

Although *The Long Good Friday* is now considered both a classic
of British and gangster cinemas, it is also a metaphor for the then

◀

**The film was made
by Handmade
Films, owned by
George Harrison,
who apparently
said he would not
have approved
the film if he
had known it was
quite so violent.**

newly formed Thatcher government. Shand delivers a speech to his esteemed guests aboard his massive yacht sailing up the Thames about the future of London and its economic development that could have come right out of a Tory Party conference. Britain is set to develop, specifically London, moving away from its colonial past and emerging as a major European nation's capital city, much as Prime Minister Margaret Thatcher

"I'LL HAVE HIS CARCASS DRIPPING BLOOD BY MIDNIGHT."

HAROLD SHAND

herself argued, but it needs to attract major investment in business partnerships in order to achieve that potential; Britain could never do it on its own. All of which would make *The Long Good Friday* a standard right-wing business melodrama if it didn't take the next step, which is to point out that all those voices praising Britain's future economic growth are actually ruthless gangsters.

The ambiguous and convoluted plot reveals, ultimately, that these attacks are revenge for a drug deal gone wrong with the IRA, and which Shand had no knowledge of in the first place. Which, should the anti-Thatcherite reading of the film be correct, suggests that this "new" Britain needs to finish cleaning up its old business (i.e., Ireland) before it can move to that golden future it wants. Unfortunately for Shand, Margaret Thatcher, and the Tory party, it first needs to contend with its existing problems and recognize its own history of exploitation. **MK**

► Bob Hoskins gives the performance of a lifetime as the menacing crook Harold Shand.

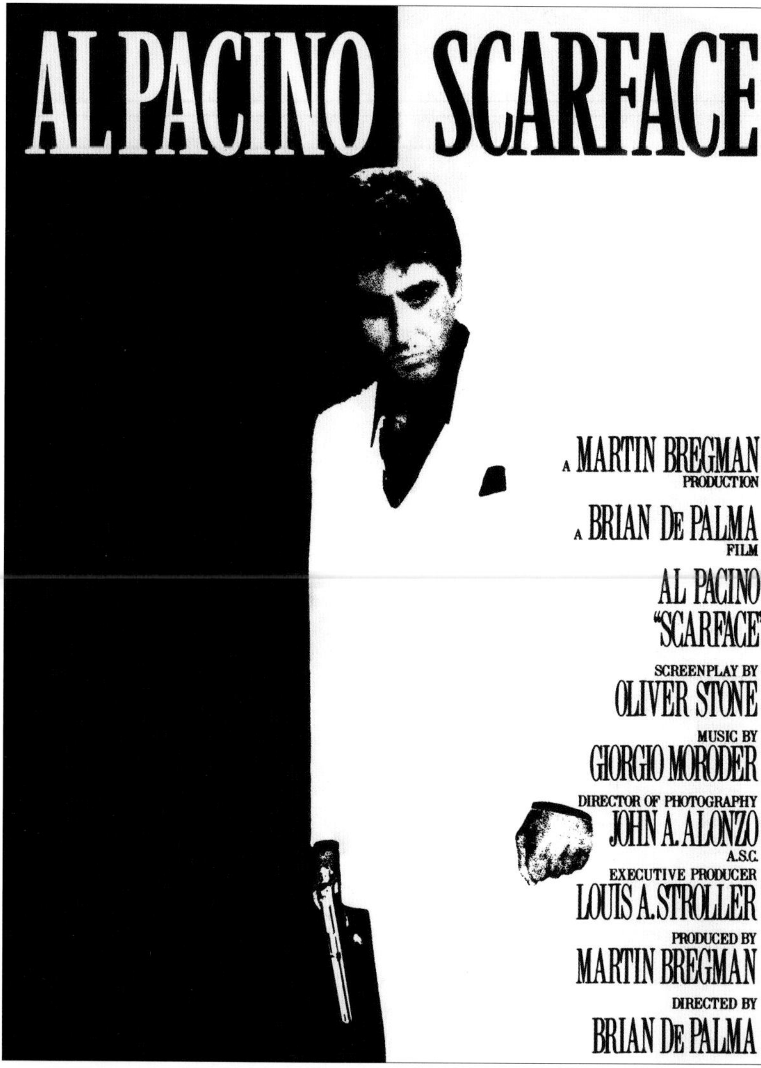

AL PACINO SCARFACE

A MARTIN BREGMAN
PRODUCTION

A BRIAN De PALMA
FILM

AL PACINO
"SCARFACE"

SCREENPLAY BY
OLIVER STONE

MUSIC BY
GIORGIO MORODER

DIRECTOR OF PHOTOGRAPHY
JOHN A. ALONZO
A.S.C.

EXECUTIVE PRODUCER
LOUIS A. STROLLER

PRODUCED BY
MARTIN BREGMAN

DIRECTED BY
BRIAN De PALMA

SCARFACE 1983 (U.S.)

Director Brian De Palma **Producer** Martin Bregman **Screenplay** Oliver Stone
Cinematography John A. Alonzo **Music** Giorgio Moroder **Cast** Al Pacino, Michelle
Pfeiffer, Steven Bauer, Mary Elizabeth Mastrantonio, Robert Loggia, Miriam Colon,
F. Murray Abraham, Paul Shenar, Harris Yulin, Ángel Salazar, Arnaldo Santana, Al Israel

Brian De Palma is one of those directors who, when they're on a
roll, make tremendous films; but unfortunately, when they're not
on a roll, their films can be almost unwatchable. And sometimes it
is hard to tell the difference. De Palma's pictures are frequently
reviled, and despite the fact that *Scarface* is now considered a
modern classic, upon its initial release in 1983 most audiences and
critics didn't seem to "get" it at all.

In 1980, Fidel Castro allowed tens of thousands of Cuban
criminals to leave the island in any way they could from Mariel
harbor. They were picked up by the American Coast Guard and
encamped in Miami. Among them is Tony Montana (Pacino), a
young Cuban who dreams the American Dream. He becomes
involved as a mobster for local Cuban gangster Frank Lopez
(Loggia), but covets Lopez's beautiful moll Elvira (Pfeiffer), as well as
his whole operation. Basically, Montana wants it all: Lopez's girl, his
drug business, his life. Although Tony eventually does get
everything he desires, it leaves him empty, paranoid, and alone.

De Palma's film is dedicated to Ben Hecht and Howard Hawks,
those Hollywood pioneers who made the original *Scarface: The
Shame of a Nation* in 1932. Ostensibly *Scarface* is a remake that

◄
**Immortalized
by the stylish
monochrome
poster, featuring
Montana (Pacino)
smoldering in his
signature white
suit, *Scarface* has
now become
a cult classic.**

keeps a few of the original's leitmotifs (like Tony's adopted motto, "The world is yours") and the basic story line. And yet, this 1983 production is probably more famous than the original. The film has developed a strong following among the hip-hop and gangsta rap cultures since its release.

Imbued with the myth of Horatio Alger, Montana lives the American Dream. As he himself famously intones, "In this country,

> ## "I ALWAYS TELL THE TRUTH. EVEN WHEN I LIE."
>
> *TONY MONTANA*

you gotta make the money first. Then when you get the money, you get the power. Then when you get the power, you get the women." But in Oliver Stone's parody of the Dream, it is an empty one—as Tony increases his wealth and power, his paranoia also increases. Self-made men may have money and power, but they have no one to share it with. Tony's ascendancy is reflected in the increasing levels of extravagance and flamboyance he shows as well as in the film's mise-en-scène, which becomes more outlandish and De Palmaesque as things wears on. The final gunfight is so extravagant and over-the-top it has become a cinematic cliché, along with the now-classic final line, "Say hello to my little friend" (actually an M16 assault rifle with an M203 40mm grenade launcher attached to the barrel). Clichés abound here, or rather it appears that way watching it now; back in 1983, *Scarface* was the movie that forged these clichés in the first place. **MK**

► Montana (Pacino) savors the excesses of the "American Dream" before plummeting into self-destruction.

ARNON MILCHAN Presents A SERGIO LEONE Film
Also Starring ROBERT De NIRO "ONCE UPON A TIME IN AMERICA"
Also Starring JAMES WOODS · ELIZABETH McGOVERN · JOE PESCI
BURT YOUNG as "Joe" · TUESDAY WELD and TREAT WILLIAMS as "Jimmy O'Donnell"

Produced by ARNON MILCHAN Directed by SERGIO LEONE

ONCE UPON A TIME IN AMERICA

1984 (ITALY • U.S.)

Director Sergio Leone **Producer** Arnon Milchan **Screenplay** Leonardo Benvenuti, Piero De Bernardi, Enrico Medioli, Franco Arcalli, Franco Ferrini, Sergio Leone
Cinematography Tonino Delli Colli **Music** Ennio Morricone **Cast** Robert De Niro, James Woods, Elizabeth McGovern, Tuesday Weld, James Hayden, William Forsythe

It is not surprising that Sergio Leone's final masterpiece, *Once Upon a Time in America*, was so heavily slated upon its American release in 1984; the film had been reedited by the producers from 229 minutes down to just under two and a half hours. Even at the almost four-hour mark, the film is tight and brisk; to edit it down by almost half must have made it utterly incomprehensible, a fact reflected in the almost unanimously negative reviews from the day. It's a vast, epic tale of the lives of four Jewish gangsters in New York, from their glory years during Prohibition through to their reunion in the late 1960s.

The film features two main narratives. The first, and based largely on Harry Grey's semi-autobiographical novel, *The Hoods*, tells of the rise of a quartet of Jewish mobsters in New York during Prohibition. These four friends, Noodles (De Niro), Max (Woods), Pasty (Hayden), and Cockeye (Forsythe), start out in their poverty-stricken childhood in Brooklyn, and emerge as gangland leaders in Manhattan during the early 1930s. The second story, by Leone himself, takes place in 1968 and revolves

◄

It reportedly took director Sergio Leone many years to persuade Harry Grey, the author of *The Hoods*, to allow him to use his book as the basis for the epic film.

around the mystery of a missing million dollars from 1933 and how Noodles was found hiding out in Buffalo for the past thirty five years. But far from being a linear plot structure, the picture is structured around a series of flashbacks as the Noodles of 1968 confronts the ghosts from his past.

Once Upon a Time in America is particularly noteworthy for Delli Colli's remarkable cinematography in evoking the

"WHEN YOU'VE BEEN BETRAYED BY A FRIEND, YOU HIT BACK."

MAXIMILIAN "MAX" BERCOVICZ

nostalgic sense of old-time Jewish Brooklyn in marvelous sepia-toned photography. These sequences from the quartet's childhood are filled with little incidental moments, like the young Patsy (Hayden) waiting for a sexual tryst, armed with his payment of a charlotte russe, only to end up eating it himself as he waits; the juxtaposition of the kids' emerging sexual maturity with the innocence of the confectionery is poignant. Ennio Morricone's BAFTA Award–winning score is possibly one of the legendary composer's most elegiac and haunting pieces of music, brilliantly highlighting the film's mood.

► **The film pulls no punches in its depictions of the carnage and consequences of brutal violence.**

While the film has a magnificent sweep, its somber essence centers on a man who is bent and broken by time, left with nothing but an impotent sadness. Leone certainly made a number of great films, and *Once Upon a Time in America* ranks up there with the very best of them. **MK**

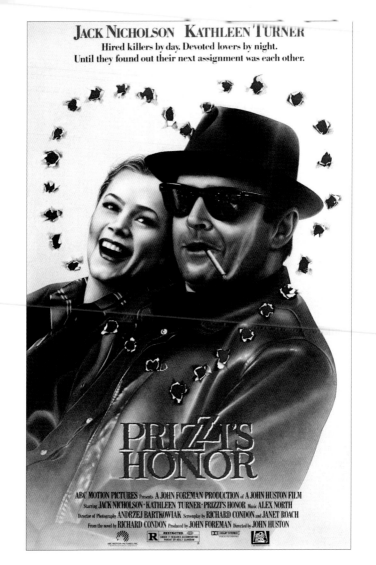

PRIZZI'S HONOR 1985 (U.S.)

Director John Huston **Producer** John Foreman **Screenplay** Richard Condon, Janet Roach **Cinematography** Andrzej Bartkowiak **Music** Alex North **Cast** Jack Nicholson, Kathleen Turner, Angelica Huston, Robert Loggia, William Hickey, John Randolph, Lee Richardson, Michael Lombard, George Santopietro, Lawrence Tierney

Director John Huston was the driving force behind *Prizzi's Honor,* based on the Richard Condon novel he greatly admired, an acerbic black comedy about the "banality of evil" that witheringly satirizes the Mafia code of obedience and honor, exposing the corrupt ruthlessness underpinning American "enterprise." Though part of Hollywood's love affair with Mafia mores, *Prizzi's Honor* differs from Coppola's grandiose *Godfather* trilogy or the farcical comedy of *Wise Guys* through Huston's expert orchestration of a sophisticated combination of gangster film, screwball comedy, and film noir, eliciting intelligent and disciplined performances from his talented cast. Huston asked Jack Nicholson to suppress his habitual quizzical intelligence, playing Charley as "simple, dumb and competent." Stuffing tissue in his upper lip, Nicholson adopted a thick Brooklyn-Italian accent, narrowed his eyes, and put on weight to create a squat, heavy look. Charley's simplicity comes from his preordained role as the Prizzis' enforcer. The film opens with his birth and adoption into the Prizzi family. Charley's role is to obey orders, a secure sense of purpose destabilized when he encounters the beautiful, sexy Irene Walker (Turner). In screwball

◄

Nicholson and Turner turned in wacky, oddball romantic leads alongside their sinister profession as hit man and hit woman.

comic fashion, their love is liberating and rebellious, with Charley delighting in her uninhibited, *outré* behavior. *Prizzi's Honor* is organized around a series of delicious ironies. Charley learns that Irene is also a professional hit woman, suspected of being part of a scam on one of the Prizzis' Las Vegas casinos, thus leaving Charley with a dilemma: "Do I ice her? Do I marry her?" Deciding to marry, Charley is amazed when Irene reveals

"MARXIE HELLER SO F*CK*N' SMART, HOW COME HE'S SO F*CK*N' DEAD?"

CHARLEY PARTANNA

she's been contracted by Charley's rival Dominic Prizzi to kill him. On a hit together, Irene shoots a police captain's wife, throwing the Prizzis' "understanding" with a corrupt police force into uproar. Charley finally agrees to restore the status quo by killing Irene, his father consoling him: "It's business, Charley." Charley is installed in overall control of the Prizzis' operations, but, in a further twist, this act is then revealed as the culmination of the subtle scheme of Dominic's daughter Maerose (a wonderful Anjelica Huston) to reinstall herself inside the family. Cleverest of the Prizzis, Maerose thus triumphs over the ostensible femme fatale, Irene, with Charley a mere pawn.

Prizzi's Honor was critically admired. Not a major box-office success, it has come to be recognized as one of John Huston's most accomplished films, whose dissection of corporate greed and corruption remains disturbingly contemporary. **ASp**

▶

Irene (Turner) shows her true colors in a film that successfully combines black comedy with heavy irony and romance.

A BETTER TOMORROW 1986 (HONG KONG)

Director John Woo **Producers** Tsui Hark, John Woo **Screenplay** Hing-Ka Chan, Suk-Wah Leun, John Woo **Cinematography** Wing-Hung Wong **Music** Joseph Koo, Ka-Fai Koo **Cast** Chow Yun-Fat, Leslie Cheung, Ti Lung, Emily Chu, Lee Chi Hung, Fui-On Shing, Kenneth Tsang, Tsui Hark, John Woo, Chi Fai Chan, San Nam Hung

A Better Tomorrow (a.k.a. *Ying hung boon sik*) is the film that changed two careers: director John Woo had made a few low-budget kung fu movies and some silly Hong Kong comedies before this, and actor Chow Yun-Fat was primarily known to Hong Kong audiences as a romantic lead in television comedies. After producer/director Tsui Hark hired both against type for *A Better Tomorrow* neither's career would ever be the same: Woo emerged as a preeminent action *auteur* and Chow as the action hero we associate him with today.

    A Better Tomorrow is a film of two halves. In the first half, Mark (Chow) and Ho (Lung) are Triad counterfeiters fast-tracking their way to the top of the Hong Kong mob, and Kit (Cheung) is a young cop trying to bring his brother Ho to justice in order to impress his father. Ho is caught during a doublecross in Taiwan, and ends up doing time. While in jail, Mark's fortunes take a nosedive after he falls out of favor because of a massacre that embarrasses his boss, and Kit's career has stalled because of the notoriety of his gangster brother. After being released, Ho tries to go straight (partially to help Kit's career) by becoming a taxi driver, and Mark has

◄

When John Woo's movie was released, it became the top-grossing film in Hong Kong cinema history.

been reduced to a two-bit mob lackey, living in poverty and working for the new Triad boss. As the new boss won't let Ho retire, Mark and Ho team up one last time to bring the boss down, this time with the reluctant help of Kit.

There is some controversy over who is responsible for the success of *A Better Tomorrow*: Tsui Hark has always claimed the success to be his as the film's producer, and claims further

"IF YOU DON'T STOP POINTING THAT GUN, YOU'LL HAVE TO USE IT."

MARK GOR

responsibility for having established the "new cool look" of this gangster movie. Woo, naturally, also claims that the style of the film is entirely his —the new kind of violence, dubbed "heroic bloodshed," characterized by balletic and hyperkinetic gunplay, slow-motion carnage, and a visual style that makes gunplay into a kind of kung fu for the 1980s, and underpinned by a strong moral center of brotherhood and loyalty. Regardless of who was responsible, the film's cool look took Hong Kong youth fashion by storm, with the city's men dressing and strutting like Mark.

▶

Mark (Yun-Fat) gets fiery. His style was seen to be so cool that the youth of Hong Kong adopted his style of black trench coats and shades.

Woo's career was at rock bottom when Tsui Hark proposed this remake of Patrick Lung's 1967 Cantonese classic movie *Story of a Discharged Prisoner*. The resulting film was responsible for the birth of the genre and certainly the genesis of many Hollywood action movies that followed. **MK**

AL CAPONE.
He ruled Chicago
with absolute power.
No one could touch him.
No one could stop him.

Until Eliot Ness
and a small force of men
swore they'd bring
him down.

THE UNTOUCHABLES

PARAMOUNT PICTURES PRESENTS AN ART LINSON PRODUCTION A BRIAN DE PALMA FILM
THE UNTOUCHABLES KEVIN COSTNER CHARLES MARTIN SMITH ANDY GARCIA
ROBERT DE NIRO as AL CAPONE and SEAN CONNERY as MALONE
Music by ENNIO MORRICONE Visual Consultant PATRIZIA VON BRANDENSTEIN Art Director WILLIAM A. ELLIOTT
Director of Photography STEPHEN H. BURUM, A.S.C. Written by DAVID MAMET Produced by ART LINSON Directed by BRIAN DE PALMA
A PARAMOUNT PICTURE

THE UNTOUCHABLES 1987 (U.S.)

Director Brian De Palma **Producer** Art Linson **Screenplay** David Mamet
Cinematography Stephen H. Burum **Music** Ennio Morricone **Cast** Kevin Costner,
Robert De Niro, Sean Connery, Andy Garcia, Charles Martin Smith, Richard Bradford,
Jack Keyhoe, Brad Sullivan, Billy Drago, Patricia Clarkson, Vito D'Ambrosio

---

From the opening notes of Ennio Morricone's magnificent
score, *The Untouchables* is spellbinding. It is a movie in which
everything works together beautifully. The acting is great, and
for once, the director's excessive style is held in check.

Based on an old and largely forgettable ABC TV series from
the early 1960s, *The Untouchables* is the story of a bland federal
agent, Elliott Ness (Costner), and his mission to stop the
flamboyant Al Capone (De Niro) any way he can. Although at
first Ness tries to play the good cop by the book, under the
tutelage of crusty police veteran Jim Malone (Connery) he
learns "the Chicago way": breaking every rule possible in order
to bring down the bad guy. Ness and Malone complete their
team of "untouchables" with brave pencil pusher Oscar Wallace
(Smith) and idealistic rookie cop George Stone (Garcia).

The film is as hackneyed and clichéd as it sounds, but
screenwriter Mamet and director De Palma fashion out of the
clichés a mythic tale of good, evil, and the birth of the FBI. Like
a classical tragedy, the picture's logic, expressed by Ness
himself, elevates The Law to almost divine status. Early on he
announces to his army of Chicago's finest that they are

◄

**Sean Connery
won the Oscar for
Best Actor in a
Supporting Role
as the world-weary
cop Jim Malone,
who is the human
element between
the evil Capone
and upright Ness.**

forbidden to take a drink, not because it is morally wrong, but simply because it is against the law (under the Volstead Act, better known as Prohibition). As the "untouchables" bring the fight to Capone's organization, one by one Ness' men give in to temptation—first Wallace, after the fight on the Canadian border, sees one of the whiskey barrels shot up and leaking booze comically, so he avails himself of a quick shot before

"MAKE SURE WHEN YOUR SHIFT IS OVER YOU GO HOME ALIVE."

JIM MALONE

killing off the rest of Capone's men. Almost the next scene sees Wallace fatally shot. Likewise, Malone surreptitiously has a bottle stashed in his apartment and he too is killed. We never see either Ness or Stone take a drink, and they live to see the end of the film. The characters' fates thus seem directly linked to their adherence to the law. Emphasizing this mythic level the film operates on, De Palma almost always photographs his heroes with low-angle camera placement, allowing these figures to dominate the screen.

▶ **The last survivor of the real "untouchables," Albert H. Wolff, advised Costner on his role as the earnest federal agent Elliot Ness.**

Although the movie is probably best remembered for De Palma's meticulous reconstruction of the Odessa Steps sequence from Eisenstein's *Battleship Potemkin* (1925), *The Untouchables* is still a film of remarkable mythic power, if a somewhat dubious ideology. As the bland but law-abiding hero triumphs at the end, so too, ultimately, does the FBI. **MK**

WHEN PEOPLE ARE AFRAID OF YOU...
YOU CAN DO ANYTHING.

REMEMBER
THAT.

THE KRAYS

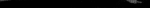

BONDED BY BLOOD

PARKFIELD ENTERTAINMENT PRESENTS A FUGITIVE FEATURES PRODUCTION OF A PETER MEDAK FILM 'THE KRAYS'
BILLIE WHITELAW • TOM BELL • GARY KEMP • MARTIN KEMP
PHOTOGRAPHY BY ALEX THOMSON MUSIC BY MICHAEL KAMEN WRITTEN BY PHILIP RIDLEY ASSOCIATE PRODUCER PAUL COWAN
EXECUTIVE PRODUCERS JIM BEACH AND MICHELE KIMCHE WITH SPECIAL THANKS TO PAUL FELDMAN

▲ PARKFIELD PRODUCED BY DOMINIC ANCIANO AND RAY BURDIS DIRECTED BY PETER MEDAK

THE KRAYS 1990 (U.K.)

Director Peter Medak **Producers** Dominic Anciano, Ray Burdis **Screenplay** Philip Ridley **Cinematography** Alex Thomson **Music** Michael Kamen **Cast** Martin Kemp, Gary Kemp, Billie Whitelaw, Tom Bell, Susan Fleetwood, Charlotte Cornwell, Kate Hardie, Avis Bunnage, Alfred Lynch, Gary Love, Steven Berkoff, Jimmy Jewel

Recounting the true story of twin British gangsters who became the most notorious gangland leaders in 1960s East End London, Peter Medak's *The Krays* is a multilayered crime drama about vicious brothers and family.

The film opens in 1933 with Violet Kray (Whitelaw) giving birth to male twins—Reginald and Ronald. As the pair grows up, it is readily apparent that the domineering Violet controls the family, and that the boys like to have tussles with kids and adults alike. In the 1960s, the adult Reggie (Martin Kemp) and Ronnie (Gary Kemp) have turned their penchant for violence into profit, having opened a series of high-end nightclubs. The duo manage to successfully keep their underworld activities hidden until they decide to deal with notorious London gangsters George Cornell (Berkoff) and Jack McVitie (Bell), resulting in a pair of assassinations that culminates with the brothers' life sentencing.

Similarly to David Cronenberg's *Dead Ringers* (1988), screenwriter Philip Ridley offers an exploration into the world of twin psychology and family ties befitting a Greek tragedy. The Kray boys are in their own insular universe and inseparable,

◄

The real-life Kray twins cooperated with the making of *The Krays,* and Reggie originally suggested that Patsy Kensit should play his wife, Frances, but in the end Kate Hardie did a fine job.

so much so that they routinely speak at the same time in their youth. Additionally, the relationships between mother and sons borders on Oedipal, as the twins will harm even their father in defense of their mom. When Reg pursues a normal life and marries Frances (Hardie), Ronald—who is bisexual—feels slighted and reacts violently. This establishes a sibling rivalry suggestive of Roman legends Remus and Romulus that is

"WE DON'T FIGHT EACH OTHER. WE STICK TOGETHER. THAT'S HOW WE'RE STRONG." *VIOLET KRAY*

repaired only when Frances commits suicide. This allows Ronald to suggest to his brother that all they have is each other, and the duo strongly reunite in an orgy of killing.

Other major themes embodied in the picture include class warfare, gangster nobility, free will, and mortality. Medak scored a casting coup with Gary and Martin Kemp, real-life brothers formerly of the '80s pop band Spandau Ballet. Both are highly effective in displaying the emotions of the deadly duo—Gary with Ronald's physical and psychological brutality, and Martin with Reggie's transitional control from his brother to his wife. Equally effective is Whitelaw as the domineering matriarch. Her presence looms over the household as the doting mother who delivers tea to criminal meetings and feels that "Men are born children and they stay children." As a result, she turns a blind eye to the criminal activity of her two brutal sons. **WW**

▶
Reggie Kray (played by Martin Kemp) gets nasty. Despite their pop background, the Kemp brothers were impressive in bringing the twins to life.

GOODFELLAS 1990 (U.S.)

Director Martin Scorsese **Producer** Irwin Winkler **Screenplay** Martin Scorsese
and Nicholas Pileggi from Pileggi's book *Wiseguys* **Cinematography** Michael Ballhaus
Music Christopher Brooks **Cast** Robert De Niro, Ray Liotta, Joe Pesci, Lorraine
Bracco, Paul Sorvino, Frank Sivero, Tony Darrow, Mike Starr, Frank Vincent, Chuck Low

An adaptation of Nicolas Pileggi's best-selling book *Wiseguys*,
Goodfellas is the true-life account of mobster and eventual
FBI informant Henry Hill. Martin Scorsese was no stranger to
the gangster film when he chose, along with Pileggi, to adapt
the life story of Hill, a half-Irish, half-Italian-American mobster.
Hill's life, as played out in the movie by Ray Liotta, was a high-
octane mix of drugs, girls, and gangland violence. Seemingly
perfect fodder for Scorsese, a director who had forged his
reputation in the early '70s with the gritty *Mean Streets* (1973),
and who would later revisit America's murky underworld in
both *Casino* (1995) and *The Departed* (2006), the film offers a
chilling glimpse into the double-crossing, two-timing, and
volatile world of the 1970s New York mob.

Despite the usual gangster film recipe of mob hits,
racketeering and FBI shakedowns, all topped off here by a
stellar cast headed by Ray Liotta, Robert De Niro, and Joe Pesci,
Goodfellas is more than just another generic gangster movie.
Hill's rapid ascent to the top of a violent world of wiseguys and
hoods is eventually shattered by petty suspicions and jealousies
that show the mob as a screwed-up blue-collar familial unit

◀
**Martin Scorsese's
hard-hitting Mafia
masterpiece uses a
camera style that is
as forceful as a gun
in the ribs.**

rather than the slick dream machine of the opening frames. *Goodfellas* received six Academy Award nominations, including Best Picture, but it was Pesci's show-stealing turn as uber-nut Tommy DeVito that would see him walk away with the film's only Academy Award in the shape of the Best Supporting Actor gong. Pesci, the most unnerving of gangsters and one with whom you most definitely wouldn't want to play poker, gives a

"THAT'S THE WAY. YOU DON'T TAKE NO SH*T FROM NOBODY."

JIMMY CONWAY

powder-keg performance as the borderline psychotic mobster DeVito. *Goodfellas* is ultimately many different things: a crime biopic, a buddy movie, a family saga, and a cautionary tale of avarice and ambition.

Stylistically, Scorsese doesn't skimp on the bravura camera work. A long tracking shot through the back entrance of the Copacabana nightclub takes Hill and his partner Karen (Bracco) through the kitchens to an exclusive table at the front of the club, and in this single free-flowing move offers a sweeping entry into the world of a wiseguy on his way up. The scene has been much imitated. Equally, the frenetic editing of the latter stages of the film, as Hill's career eventually spectacularly and unpredictably spirals out of control into cocaine abuse and ratting out his former friends, merely demonstrates what a house of cards his whole existence really was. **ReH**

► De Niro, Pesci, Liotta, (and victim) are mobsters whose careers of crime we follow from 1955 into the late 1970s.

KING OF NEW YORK 1990 (ITALY • U.S. • U.K.)

Director Abel Ferrara **Screenplay** Nicholas St. John **Producers** Augusto Caminito, Mary Kane **Cinematography** Bojan Bazelli **Music** Joe Delia **Cast** Christopher Walken, David Caruso, Laurence Fishburne, Victor Argo, Wesley Snipes, Janet Julian, Joey Chin, Giancarlo Esposito, Paul Calderon, Steve Buscemi, Theresa Randle

Abel Ferrara is one of the most underrated filmmakers in U.S. cinema, far more appreciated in Europe, where his sensibilities seem to resonate more profoundly. This is not to say that Ferrara has slipped completely under the radar in his home country; films like *Ms. 45* (1981), *Bad Lieutenant* (1992), *Dangerous Game* (1993), and *The Funeral* (1996) made a fleeting cause célèbre among devotees of independent cinema. However, it is 1990's *King of New York* that has achieved cult status. Like Brian De Palma's 1983 film *Scarface*—with which it shares a penchant for extremely violent set pieces and rapid-fire profanity—*King of New York* has become a canonical text among the gangster rap community. Schooly-D, who also contributed to Ferrara's *Bad Lieutenant*, *The Addiction* (1995), *New Rose Hotel* (1998), and *'R Xmas* (2001), composed much of the score.

King of New York tells the story of Frank White (Walken), a career criminal on parole from prison who declares himself "reformed." White reveals himself to be a complicated paradoxical character whose desire to "do something good" conflicts with his predilection toward violence—though, as he states, "I never killed anybody who didn't deserve it." White,

◄

Designer brutality and a fair splattering of foul-mouthed expletives signaled Abel Ferrara's foray into the big-budget gangster genre.

whose very name suggests both a raw, base humanity, and a kind of transcendental purity, is a morally conflicted Robin Hood figure whose bourgeois pretensions complicate how we understand his altruistic pretensions. For example, he uses money stolen from the drug lords for whose deaths he is responsible to subsidize a failing South Bronx hospital, punishes criminals responsible for the exploitation of labor (primarily

"YOU GUYS GOT FAT WHILE EVERYBODY STARVED ON THE STREET. NOW IT'S MY TURN." *FRANK WHITE*

immigrant workers), and shows no mercy toward those who would profit from child prostitution. In this sense, White is the prototypical Ferrara hero, a protagonist in spiritual crisis, searching for forgiveness and redemption in a violent milieu in which souls, like bodies, are ripe for destruction.

Cinematically, *King of New York* is one of Ferrara's most carefully constructed films with its meticulously composed scenes, revealing a formalism accentuated by chiaroscuro and Rembrandt-style lighting to achieve emotional impact. Ferrara's depiction of New York City at night is particularly memorable, with its mist-enshrouded streets bathed in an ethereal blue light. Equally praised and excoriated upon its initial release, *King of New York* is a highly recommended entry point for audiences looking to familiarize themselves with one of the United States' most overlooked and woefully misunderstood directors. **JM**

▶
New York's underbelly of treacherous black and Hispanic gangs is ripped open in this murderous tale. Laurence Fishburne plays the hood Jimmy Jump.

"NOT SINCE 'THE GODFATHER'
HAS THERE BEEN A PORTRAIT OF GANGSTERISM
AS POWERFUL AS THIS AUDACIOUS, ELECTRIFYING
MASTERPIECE FROM THE COEN BROTHERS."
—GUY FLATLEY, COSMOPOLITAN

FROM JOEL COEN AND ETHAN COEN,
THE CREATORS OF
"BLOOD SIMPLE" AND "RAISING ARIZONA"

MILLER'S CROSSING

CIRCLE FILMS PRESENTS A TED AND JIM PEDAS/BEN BARENHOLTZ/BILL DURKIN PRODUCTION GABRIEL BYRNE
MARCIA GAY HARDEN JOHN TURTURRO JON POLITO J.E. FREEMAN AND ALBERT FINNEY "MILLER'S CROSSING"
EDITED BY MICHAEL MILLER PRODUCTION DESIGNER DENNIS GASSNER DIRECTOR OF PHOTOGRAPHY BARRY SONNENFELD MUSIC BY CARTER BURWELL EXECUTIVE PRODUCER BEN BARENHOLTZ
CO-PRODUCER GRAHAM PLACE CO-PRODUCER MARK SILVERMAN WRITTEN BY JOEL COEN & ETHAN COEN
PRODUCED BY ETHAN COEN DIRECTED BY JOEL COEN

MILLER'S CROSSING 1990 (U.S.)

Director Joel Coen **Producer** Ethan Coen **Screenplay** Joel Coen, Ethan Coen
Cinematography Barry Sonnenfield **Music** Carter Burwell **Cast** Gabriel Byrne,
John Turturro, Marcia Gay Harden, Albert Finney, Jon Polito, J. E. Freeman, Mike Starr,
Al Mancini, Richard Woods, Thomas Toner, Steve Buscemi, Mario Todisco, Olek Krupa

A meticulously constructed revisionist genre film, *Miller's Crossing*
is unofficially based upon Dashiell Hammett's novels *The Glass
Key* and *Red Harvest*. Gabriel Byrne stars as Tom Regan, right-
hand man of Irish mob boss Leo O'Bannion (Finney) who rules
over an unnamed "eastern city" in the 1920s Prohibition era.

Trouble arises when rival gangster Johnny Caspar (Polito)
asks Leo's permission to whack Bernie Bernbaum (Turturro)—a
small-time crook who is profiting from Caspar's fixed fights
while paying protection money to Leo. Against Tom's advice
and because of his relationship with Bernie's sister Verna
(Harden), Leo refuses to sanction the murder and this ignites a
war between the rival gangs. Tom is thrown out of Leo's mob
when he reveals his own relationship with Verna and, with
nowhere else to go, joins the increasingly powerful Caspar. To
prove his allegiance, Tom must now kill Bernie himself. When
the moment arrives and he finds they are alone, Tom spares
Bernie's life and sends him into hiding, but the lack of witnesses
draws suspicion from Caspar's henchman Eddie Dane
(Freeman). The double-crossing and violence escalates until
Caspar's gang begins to self-destruct and, having outsmarted

◄

**The Coen
brothers ventured
successfully
into traditional
gangster territory,
especially with
their use of
muted colors and
brooding overcast
weather giving
the forest scenes
a painterly quality.**

them all, only Tom survives. At Bernie's funeral Verna makes it clear she's through with Tom and Leo invites him to come back, but he declines and walks away.

Miller's Crossing emanates a hard-boiled authenticity that is owing in part to the Coens' superbly crafted pulp film dialogue. When Tom asks, "What's the rumpus?" and Caspar (sensing disrespect) asks if you're giving him the high hat, the picture is

"THE MOVIE IS A GANGSTER STORY ... BUT THE CHARACTERS, THE MORALITY, HAVE A MORE UNIVERSAL APPLICATION." E. COEN

channeling the genre's literary incarnation and a style of dialogue perfected by writers like Hammett and later, Chandler. The film's shadowy aesthetic grows from conscientious study of film noir semantics and from the Coens' acute, obsessive cinephilia. A number of scenes, however, take us beyond the city into spaces less characteristic of the classical noir and gangster genres; Bernie's supposed execution in the forest re-creates, in terms of both location and color palate, the extraordinary murder scene in Bernardo Bertolucci's *The Conformist* (1970).

► John Turturro based his performance of Bernie Bernbaum on the film's cinematographer, Barry Sonnenfield.

Although the film's overt stylization has drawn the bulk of critical focus, the Coens maintain that *Miller's Crossing* is primarily about ethics. Tom spends much of the movie masterminding and double-crossing, but he is driven by his own complex, contradictory code of ethics and a subjective understanding of what is true and right. **AK**

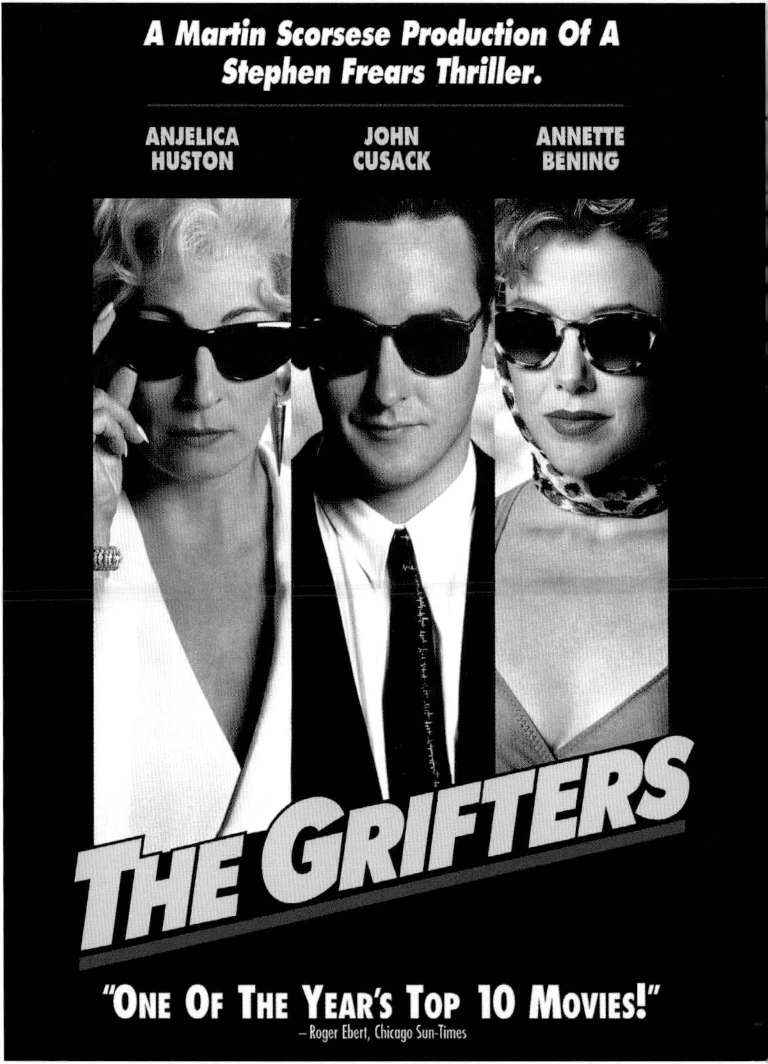
A Martin Scorsese Production Of A
Stephen Frears Thriller.
ANJELICA HUSTON
JOHN CUSACK
ANNETTE BENING
THE GRIFTERS
"ONE OF THE YEAR'S TOP 10 MOVIES!"
– Roger Ebert, Chicago Sun-Times

THE GRIFTERS 1990 (U.S.)

Director Stephen Frears **Producers** Robert A. Harris, Jim Painter, Martin Scorsese
Screenplay Donald E. Westlake **Cinematography** Oliver Stapleton **Music** Elmer
Bernstein **Cast** John Cusack, Anjelica Huston, Annette Bening, Pat Hingle, J. T. Walsh,
Charles Napier, Jan Munroe, Stephen Tobolowsky, Robert Weems, Henry Jones

Like a deft pickpocket that sneaks up on you, *The Grifters* subtly
brings to life the colorful underworld of con artists as three
characters try to work their craft on each other. Roy (Cusack) is
a master swindler who underutilizes his top game in small
actions ("short cons") to keep off the radar. On Roy's periphery
is Myra (Bening), a spacey love interest who is actually a high-
profile con artist maintaining this façade to bait her potential
victims. All of this changes when Lilly (Huston), Roy's mother,
enters the picture. Sent to Los Angeles to work the horse races
for gangster Bobo (Hingle), Lilly pays a visit to her estranged
son, who is at death's door after being on the wrong end of a
baseball bat during a cheat gone wrong. Soon, all three realize
there is potential in each other while "on the grift."

One of the best adaptations of the hard-boiled novels of Jim
Thompson, *The Grifters* benefits from a sharp script by
celebrated crime novelist Donald E. Westlake that retains the
source's pulpy spirit in both dialogue and action. The story
unfolds with a series of multiple deceptions—every character
working their own personal con—and maintains a nihilistic
outlook with the lonely, paranoid, and empty life of a fraudster.

◀

**The con is on with
this trio of stylish
schemers, ably
directed by British
director Frears
for his first foray
in America.**

The film also brilliantly highlights the art and addiction of the con, from Cusack's subtle sleight-of-hand money tricks to Bening's description of an elaborate sting on a wealthy businessman (Napier).

The script establishes man's immense capacity for greed within the film's heart by exploring the dysfunctional mother/son relationship between Lilly and Roy. Echoing themes of

"YOU'RE WORKING SOME ANGLE AND DON'T TELL ME YOU'RE NOT 'CAUSE I WROTE THE BOOK." LILLY

Greek tragedy, there is a sexual tension between the pair, so much so that viewers initially wonder if Lilly is only a figurative "mother" to Roy in the con game. The relationship builds to an inevitable finish where Lilly ultimately uses her sexuality in an attempt to con her own son. The allure of the con is so strong that, in the end, Lilly weeps briefly for the son she has killed before stealing his cash.

Utilizing stylistic elements from several different decades, Frears successfully created a timeless period that pays homage to the film noir style while reversing it with a concentration on bright colors and graphic violence. The three leads form a compelling triangle of people who are all living on the edge, resulting in a pair of Oscar nominations for the two femmes fatales, Huston and Bening, and further establishing Cusack as an actor of dramatic accomplishment. **WW**

► **Anjelica Huston as Lilly, the ruthless survivor and con artist, gives a performance of almost Greek Tragedy proportions.**

WESLEY SNIPES ICE-T MARIO VAN PEEBLES JUDD NELSON
Where survival depends on friends, trust and power... An organized crime family out to run this city is up against cops who know its streets.
NEW JACK CITY
WARNER BROS.
JACKSON/McHENRY "NEW JACK CITY" WESLEY SNIPES ICE T CHRIS ROCK
MARIO VAN PEEBLES JUDD NELSON STEVEN KEMPER CHARLES C. BENNETT
FRANCIS KENNY PRESTON L. HOLMES MICHEL COLOMBIER
THOMAS LEE WRIGHT THOMAS LEE WRIGHT BARRY MICHAEL COOPER
R RESTRICTED
DOUG McHENRY GEORGE JACKSON MARIO VAN PEEBLES
DOLBY STEREO
WARNER BROS

NEW JACK CITY 1991 (U.S.)

Director Mario Van Peebles **Producers** George Jackson, Doug McHenry
Screenplay Thomas Lee Wright, Barry Michael Cooper **Cinematography** Francis
Kenny **Music** Vassal Benford, Michel Colombier **Cast** Wesley Snipes, Ice-T, Allen
Payne, Mario Van Peebles, Judd Nelson, Chris Rock, Michael Michele, Bill Nunn

New Jack City is the directorial debut of Mario Van Peebles, son
of director Melvin Van Peebles whose *Sweet Sweetback's
Badasss Song* (1971) was the initial spark in the early
Blaxploitation movement. Its release in 1991 came at a time
when the African American population was criminally
underrepresented in the (U.S.) Hollywood-led movie industry,
and its success meant it was soon followed in quick succession
by both *Boyz N the Hood* (1991) and *Juice* (1992).

Van Peebles enlists controversial gangster rapper Ice-T, rising
stars Wesley Snipes and Chris Rock, as well as taking a role
himself, to tell the story of the Cash Money Brothers, a ruthless,
well-organized New York City drug cartel run by gang member–
turned–entrepreneur Nino Brown (Snipes). The organization's
willingness to annihilate rivals, and anyone else who attempts
to stunt their growth, echoes that of real-life drug gang the
Chambers Brothers, with whom writer Barry Michael Cooper
became fascinated after covering their story as a journalist.

The message here is anti-drugs but the movie manages to
avoid being patronizing or preaching to the viewer. Although
the rise of the Cash Money Brothers is rapid and their newly

◄
**The rise and fall
of a mobster, only
this time from
a Blaxploitation
viewpoint. Wesley
Snipes is yet
another "king
of New York."**

glamorous lifestyle is shown through somewhat of a showbiz veneer, Nino's paranoia, egomania, and psychosis soon turns their lavish boardroom into a place of intimidation, fear, and betrayal. After a number of unsuccessful attempts to bring Nino to justice, rebellious cop Scotty (Ice-T) goes undercover to ensure the equally rapid downfall of the organization and its hold over the drug-dependent masses of the neighborhoods it exploited.

"MONEY TALKS, AND BULLSH*T RUNS A MARATHON. SO, SEE YA AND I WOULDN'T WANT TO BE YA." NINO BROWN

Clearly indebted to classics of the gangster genre such as *White Heat* (1949), *The Godfather* (1972), and *Scarface* (1983), one memorable scene begins with Nino laughing as he watches Scarface's demise on television. Surrounded by women, food, and wine, Nino's arrogance has begun to cloud his judgment and he soon begins to slip, eventually losing control of the empire he fought so ruthlessly to build.

Whereas later releases such as *Menace II Society* (1994) walk a fine line between social commentary and exploitation flick, *New Jack City* arrived at a time when black filmmakers were determined to depict life in the deprived inner-city areas of America without glamorizing the gangster lifestyle. The movie leans toward anti-capitalism throughout, clearly showing in Nino Brown the ill fate that awaits the individual who chooses to pursue his own advancement at the expense of his community. **MW**

► Streetwise cop Appleton (Ice-T) closes in on ruthless Nino Brown's (Snipes) domain, with his disaffected partner Peretti (Nelson).

"★★★★
One of the best
films of recent years."
— Roger Ebert, CHICAGO SUN-TIMES

ICE CUBE · CUBA GOODING, JR. · MORRIS CHESTNUT AND LARRY FISHBURNE AS FURIOUS

BOYZ N THE HOOD 1991 (U.S.)

Director John Singleton **Producer** Steve Nicolaides **Screenplay** John Singleton
Cinematography Charles Mills **Music** Stanley Clarke **Cast** Ice Cube, Cuba Gooding
Jr., Morris Chestnut, Lawrence Fishburne, Nia Long, Tyra Ferrell, Angela Bassett,
John Cothran Jr., Kareem J. Grimes, Tammy Hanson, Regina King, Dedrick D. Gobert

While *Boyz N the Hood* was one of the first of the spate of early
'90s 'hood films to dominate cinema screens, and despite the
obvious narrative focus on the gangsta culture of South-Central
Los Angeles, crime and violence are not this film's central
themes; this is not really an African American version of *Mean
Streets* (1973), for example.

Boyz N the Hood focuses on Tre Styles (Gooding Jr.), a smart
and hardworking young black man who has just passed his
SATs and is getting ready to start college in the fall. He lives with
his father, Furious (Fishburne), a financial consultant in the
community who believes strongly in empowering African
Americans through economic emancipation. Tre is further
supported by his friends Ricky (Chestnut), a promising athlete
with a football scholarship, and Ricky's brother Doughboy
(Cube), a malt-liquor drinking homeboy who knows he's going
to die on the streets of the 'hood.

Unlike some of the other 'hood films to have emerged in this
period (nor to denigrate those other ones), *Boyz N the Hood* is
not a gangsta film as much as it is a coming-of-age film for
young Tre. Furious raises him to be a proud and respectful

◄

In this coming-
of-age movie
and snapshot of
L.A. gang culture
in the 1980s,
Singleton gives
clear direction
to his talented
African American
ensemble.

member of the African American community, teaching him to "look people in the eye" and to "never respect someone who doesn't respect you". Singleton's movie is highly didactic; Furious's messages to Tre are also messages to the young black men in the audience, teaching them how to be respectful and proud. Brandi (Long), Tre's longtime girlfriend, functions more as a moral temptation for Tre than as a three-dimensional

"THERE ARE NO CHEAP SHOTS, NOTHING IS THROWN IN FOR EFFECT."

MOVIE CRITIC AND AUTHOR ROGER EBERT

character in her own right. As a staunch Roman Catholic, she refuses to have sex with him until after marriage. Although the two do end up in bed together, Brandi teaches Tre that respect is the key to any successful relationship. Brandi is, in the long run, another test to ensure Tre's success in becoming a man.

The tragedy in the film is the drive-by shooting of Ricky, murdering him and his family's hopes of seeing one of them go to college. Although the shooting isn't exactly random—Ricky had upset another gangbanger by talking back to him—his death underlies just how dangerous the world of South-Central is; simply talking back to someone can get you murdered there. One hopes that Singleton's lessons to his audience were taken aboard, but in the wake of other, more sensational gangsta films like *Menace II Society* (1993), one fears the message may have got lost amid all the drive-by shootings. **MK**

► Tre lives with his father, shown here the aptly named Furious, played by Laurence Fishburne.

GLAMOUR
WAS THE
DISGUISE.

WARREN BEATTY · ANNETTE BENING

A BARRY LEVINSON FILM

BUGSY

TriStar Pictures PRESENTS A MULHOLLAND PRODUCTIONS/BALTIMORE PICTURES PRODUCTION
WARREN BEATTY ANNETTE BENING A BARRY LEVINSON FILM "BUGSY" HARVEY KEITEL BEN KINGSLEY AND JOE MANTEGNA
EDITED BY ALBERT WOLSKY MUSIC BY ENNIO MORRICONE PRODUCTION DESIGNER DENNIS GASSNER DIRECTOR OF PHOTOGRAPHY ALLEN DAVIAU, A.S.C. WRITTEN BY JAMES TOBACK
PRODUCED BY MARK JOHNSON, BARRY LEVINSON AND WARREN BEATTY DIRECTED BY BARRY LEVINSON

BUGSY 1991 (U.S.)

Director Barry Levinson **Producers** Warren Beatty, Mark Johnson, Barry Levinson **Screenplay** James Toback (from the book by Dean Jennings) **Cinematography** Allen Daviau **Music** Ennio Morricone **Cast** Warren Beatty, Annette Bening, Harvey Keitel, Ben Kingsley, Elliot Gould, Joe Mantegna

Noteworthy for the lavish and glamorous array of Hollywood fashion and scenery, and for its nods to cinematic clichés (perhaps most prominently in the *Casablanca*-esque goodbye scene), *Bugsy* brings to life the Las Vegas dream of money, success, and extravagance, albeit through the eccentric and maniacal mind of entrepreneur Benjamin "Bugsy" Siegel (Beatty).

A status seeker and an industrious man of ideas, and yet all the while a dreamer and self-deceiver, Ben is an unrelenting social networker and fastidious self-improver (privately he repeatedly recites the line "Twenty dwarfs took turns doing handstands on the carpet"), although there is an underlying darkness in his character: a ruthless killer disposing of those standing in his way. Yet Ben is such an utterly exaggerated, larger-than-life character that there is farcicality to his ruthlessness and to the ways in which he enacts his unending quest for accomplishment. In one notable scene he reprimands an underling by forcing him to behave like a farmyard animal on his hands and knees.

The essence of Ben's character is captured in an experience accentuated to one of visionary proportions by director Barry Levinson: an epiphany of what would later become the

◄
The movie won Oscars for Best Art Direction and Best Costume Design, and it goes without saying that Beatty and Bening are a class act together on- and off-screen.

Flamingo casino. Though Ben subsequently devoted much of his life to the design, financing, and construction of the Flamingo, the conflict between these two sides to his character—the dreamer and the perfectionist—continues to plague the realization of the vision he had that day while driving through the Nevada desert. Although his perfectionism is manifested in hard work and in hard-fought relations with

"EVERYBODY DESERVES A FRESH START EVERY ONCE IN A WHILE."

BENJAMIN "BUGSY" SIEGEL

dignitaries and businessmen, Ben is detached from reality in a variety of ways. He experiences fantasies of love, success, and wealth, borrowing more and more, building up huge debts in order to finance the Flamingo, pretending to be rich to impress those around him. Although he endures a loveless marriage, and despite numerous affairs, Ben blindly revels in his family man status, unwilling or perhaps unable to recognize the unhappy reality of his situation. Eventually he neglects his family and falls in love with small-time actress Virginia Hill (Bening), although ultimately leaving his wife is almost too difficult for him to bear and his subsequent obsessive love for Virginia is presented as too fantastical. Perhaps his one genuine relationship is with friend and business associate Meyer Lansky (Kingsley), who defends Ben against his detractors throughout the much troubled construction of the Flamingo. **SR**

► **Warren Beatty produced the stylish and stylized movie and acted as Bugsy Siegel.**

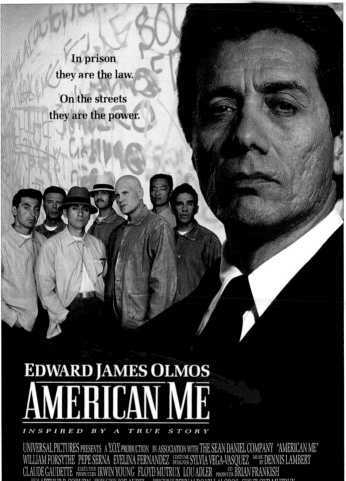

AMERICAN ME 1992 (U.S.)

Director Edward James Olmos **Producers** Sean Daniel, Robert M. Young, Edward James Olmos **Screenplay** Floyd Mutrux, Desmond Nakano **Cinematography** Reynaldo Villalobos **Music** Claude Gaudette, Dennis Lambert **Cast** Edward James Olmos, Evalina Fernández, William Forsythe

Inspired by real events and people, *American Me* is an expertly crafted tale that chronicles three decades in the life of a Mexican American gangster in Los Angeles and his rise to power in the Mexican Mafia ("La Eme").

The film centers on Montoya Santana (Olmos), a youngster growing up in the Mexican ghetto of L.A. The first half of the film follows Santana and his crew as a quick stint in juvenile detention turns into a hard-time stretch at Folsom State Prison. Here, the grown-up Santana runs the prison's gang activity alongside Caucasian partner JD (Forsythe). Despite incarceration, Santana maintains tight control of events taking place on the outside. It is once in the free world that Santana is offered a glimpse of a life he has never known in the form of Julie (Fernández).

Unlike most Hollywood-produced gangland films, *American Me* benefits from a deep attention to detail as Olmos accurately depicts the rituals, traditions, and vernacular of La Eme. The film clearly respects but rarely glamorizes the gang lifestyle. Instead it is a cautionary tale that never holds back in its realistic depiction of violence and its effect on the community. The prison section—where Olmos was given unprecedented

◄

The Mexican Mafia, who had allegedly agreed to the movie because they thought it would be flattering, went into apoplexy when the release revealed a very unpleasant portrait.

access to facilities and real prisoners—is the most enlightening one of the film. Drug smuggling, assassinations, gang boundaries, power, and respect—all aspects are examined while keeping the human element at the forefront. The resulting condemnation is that the prison system is a place that breeds criminal activity rather than inhibiting it.

The film produces a response in the second half with

"THERE WAS NOTHING THE SYSTEM COULD DO TO STOP ME."

MONTOYA SANTANA

Santana's developing relationship with Julie and deteriorating relationship with his father. This is where the heart of *American Me* lies as Santana, having grown up in institutions, finds the idea of love foreign and frightening. As Julie remarks late in the film, Santana is effectively two separate people, and the schizophrenic balancing act of love and gang life eventually causes his downfall and return to prison, where his followers now consider him weak.

Olmos' philosophy at the end of the picture seems two-fold—Julie appears to be furthering her education and looking to get out of the ghetto, yet a pessimistic coda involving a young boy induced to do a drive-by suggests a cyclical effect in the gang lifestyle and community that can no longer be undone. *American Me* conveys an honest portrayal of lives lived by many without the hope of education or prosperity. **WW**

► Gritty Mexican actor Edward James Olmos, a long way from *Battlestar Galactica*.

A JOHN WOO FILM

HARD-BOILED

CHOW YUN-FAT
周潤發

TONY LEUNG
梁朝偉

辣手神探

吳宇森作品

MAPLE GROUP HOSPITAL

GOLDEN PRINCESS PRESENTS A MILESTONE PICTURES PRODUCTION A JOHN WOO FILM
CHOW YUN-FAT . TONY LEUNG " HARD-BOILED " TERESA MO . PHILIP CHAN
CHEUNG JUE-LUH . ANTHONY WONG . BOWIE LAM & Y. YONEMURA
ORIGINAL STORY JOHN WOO SCREENPLAY BY BARRY WONG . PRODUCTION DESIGNER JAMES LEUNG
ACTION CO-ORDINATOR CHEUNG JUE-LUH DIRECTOR OF PHOTOGRAPHY WANG WING-HENG H.K.S.C
EDITED BY DAVID WU . KAI KIT-WAI & JOHN WOO MUSIC BY MICHAEL GIBBS
ASSOCIATE PRODUCER AMY CHIN PRODUCED BY LINDA KUK & TERENCE CHANG DIRECTED BY JOHN WOO

HARD-BOILED 1992 (HONG KONG)

Director John Woo **Producers** Terence Chang, Linda Kuk **Screenplay** Barry Wong, Gordon Chan, John Woo (story) **Cinematography** Wing-Hung Wong **Music** Michael Gibbs **Cast** Chow Yun-Fat, Tony Leung, Teresa Mo, Philip Chan, Anthony Wong, Hoi-Shan Kwan, Philip Kwok, Bowie Lam, Tung Wai, Johnson Law

In the early 1990s, the hyperkinetic action movies coming out of Hong Kong at that time made Hollywood action films pale by comparison. *Hard-Boiled* (a.k.a. *Lat sau san taam*) was a classic of the genre. Directed by John Woo, who had previously made *The Killer* (1989)—an extremely violent, positively demented thriller—and other works of "heroic bloodshed," *Hard-Boiled* just left all his previous movies in the dust. A supercharged thriller, starring the already legendary Yun-Fat Chow, the movie hit paydirt in Hollywood. The film features his characteristic flamboyant cinematic style, with spectacular stunts, slow-motion replays, and gory shoot-outs. Incredibly violent—with a body count in the hundreds—Woo also introduced a new vein of anarchic humor into the film. *Hard-Boiled*, together with *The Killer*, gained him a cult reputation in Hollywood, and his style was much imitated.

Hard-Boiled tells of Tequila (Chow Yun-Fat), a hard-boiled Hong Kong cop who is tracking down a massive shipment of illegal arms the Triads are moving. He runs afoul of Tony (Leung), seemingly the trusted Triad lieutenant but actually an undercover police officer. Discovering that the arms cache

◄

By the time he had finished *Hard-Boiled*, Woo had emerged as an auteur and the creator of a new genre. Embraced by Hollywood, he went on to make *Face/Off* (1997).

is being held in a specially designed basement bunker in a hospital, Tequila and Tony join forces to defeat the evil Triad boss, Johnny Wong (Wong).

As with most Hong Kong action films, specifically the work of Woo, the story is second to the over-the-top and balletic action sequences. The choreography is stunning, and some of the action scenes were even improvised, such as the famous

"YOU KNOW WHAT I HATE? . . . F*CK*NG COPS AND CREEPS WHO BETRAY THEIR OLD BOSSES." MAD DOG

staircase scene. Rumor has it that Woo and producer Tsui Hark had one of their many fallings-out over the use of music in *The Killer*: Woo wanted jazz to feature on the soundtrack, but Hark insisted on canton-pop, as he felt that Chinese audiences don't like jazz. Woo may have lost the battle on *The Killer*, but got his own back by having Tequila in *Hard-Boiled* play clarinet in a jazz trio during his off times. Woo's use of jazz in the film gives it a noirish quality, harkening back to American popular culture of the 1940s.

Some critics have suggested that *Hard Boiled* was intended by Woo to be his audition for a more lucrative Hollywood career. However, watching the movie, it seems more to be a self-conscious swan song to his Hong Kong career—a culmination of his previous work. Either way, it stands out as the final word in Hong Kong heroic bloodshed cinema. **MK**

▶
Yun-Fat Chow looks hard-boiled. During the making of the picture, more than 200 guns and over 100,000 rounds of blank ammunition were allegedly used.

RESERVOIR DOGS 1992 (U.S.)

Director Quentin Tarantino **Producer** Lawrence Bender **Screenplay** Quentin Tarantino **Cinematography** Andrzej Sekula **Music** Kathy Nelson, Karyn Rachtman **Cast** Harvey Keitel, Tim Roth, Steve Buscemi, Michael Madsen, Chris Penn, Lawrence Tierney, Quentin Tarantino, Eddie Bunker, Randy Brooks, Kirk Baltz, Steven Wright

---

It is hard to appreciate the impact of Quentin Tarantino's reinvention of pulp cinema that this film heralded on its initial release. For a debut feature, *Reservoir Dogs* announced, in no subtle way, the arrival of a brilliant new auteur.

Basically, *Reservoir Dogs* is a heist movie that never shows the heist. Six men are recruited by mobster Joe Cabot (Tierney) and his son Nice Guy Eddie (the late Penn) to steal a stock of diamonds. Each of the men are given colored code names: Mr. White (Keitel), Mr. Orange (Roth), Mr. Pink (Buscemi), Mr. Blonde (Madsen), Mr. Brown (Tarantino), and Mr. Blue (Bunker). Forbidden to give each other their real names or any details about themselves, their heist goes wrong. The police show up. Carnage ensues. Most of the action takes place at the rendezvous site; Orange has been shot in the stomach and is being comforted by White. Unbeknownst to each other, Orange is actually an undercover cop who was trying to crack Joe's gang. Although everyone suspects that there is a rat in the organization, no one knows who, with Orange above suspicion because of his mortal injury. Beyond the film's intense and graphic violence is the assured direction and writing of

◄

Tarantino, one of the most influential directors to emerge in the 1990s, burst onto the scene with this brilliant, blood-soaked take on the heist-gone-wrong, heralding a whole new brand of violent films.

newcomer Tarantino; he is audacious enough to reduce the dialogue from (what should be) important plot information to discussions of the real meaning in Madonna's song "Like a Virgin." Tarantino was a largely self-taught filmmaker/screenwriter, learning the codes and conventions from being a tremendous movie buff rather than from going to film school. That assuredness comes through in his not only conforming to

> ## "I DON'T WANNA KILL ANYBODY. BUT . . . ONE WAY OR THE OTHER, YOU'RE GETTIN' OUTTA MY WAY." *MR. PINK*

the conventions of the heist genre, but in also deftly *breaking* those conventions without a second thought. The heist is ultimately irrelevant here, as is the question of who the rat is in their midst. What emerges in *Reservoir Dogs* are the central relationships between the men themselves. Much of the screen time is spent discussing issues of honor and professionalism among thieves; these are two virtues this particular community holds in the highest esteem. The informant in their midst is a violation and betrayal of their very code. Orange and White's bonding becomes particularly profound in this regard; White stakes his professional reputation on Orange being kosher. Revealing Orange as the cop is the ultimate betrayal, and Keitel's guttural moans as he kills Orange are those of a man whose soul has been torn from his body. The final shoot-out is a spectacular gore-fest. **MK**

▶
Color-coded crooks Mr. Pink (Buscemi), on the floor, and Mr. White (Keitel).

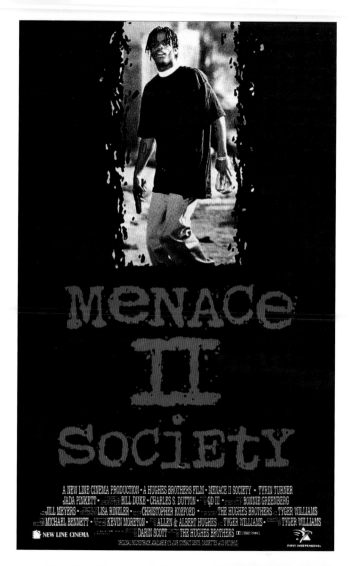

MENACE II SOCIETY 1993 (U.S.)

Directors Allen Hughes, Albert Hughes **Producer** Darin Scott **Screenplay** Tyger Williams, Allen Hughes, Albert Hughes **Cinematography** Lisa Rinzler **Music** Quincy Jones III (as QD III) **Cast** Tyrin Turner, Larenz Tate, June Kyoto Lu, Toshi Toda, Samuel L. Jackson, Anthony Johnson, Jada Pinkett, Brandon Hammond, Glenn Plummer

You might be forgiven for thinking that there was no hope for black youth in the American ghettos after watching the violent *Menace II Society* for an hour and a half. But that's not to say that this film isn't an excellent piece of realist American ghetto cinema. The camera work, score, and performances are handled with considerable flair by the young directors.

The film centers on Caine (Turner), a young man growing up in Watts in the early 1990s. His father, Tat (Jackson), was the neighborhood drug dealer, and his mother a junkie. Kane grows up in a hopeless environment of violence and drugs, but somehow manages to survive high school. *Menace II Society* takes place during the summer Caine graduates, with his whole life before him—but it is impossible for him to escape the ties of the ghetto.

Identical twin wunderkind directors Allen and Albert Hughes know their subject matter. Born in Detroit, the pair grew up in a middle-class neighborhood in Pomona, California, where the violence of the film happens blocks, or even a few houses, away from their own. "Every character is either a friend of ours, or a combination of someone we know," Allen has said

◄

Menace II Society was a directorial first for the twin brothers Allen and Albert Hughes. The movie received acclaim for its harsh and uncompromising view of inner-city violence.

in interviews. "Some of our close friends are like that. One of the guys who plays in the film . . . he did everything Caine did —he positively did. But he's cool now. He's a good guy." The twins went so far as to shoot in South-Central L.A., hiring local gang members as security and extras on the set.

Ultimately, *Menace II Society* is a profoundly existentialist film, rather than an "essentialist" one. It doesn't throw up its hands in

"NOW O-DOG WAS THE CRAZIEST NIGGA ALIVE. AMERICA'S NIGHTMARE. YOUNG, BLACK, AND DIDN'T GIVE A F*CK." *CAINE*

exploitation glory and say, much like Caine's best friend O-Dog (Tate) does, and ask, "What are you going to do? It's the hood!" This is not a movie that says ghetto violence is inescapable and essential to the culture because of the conditions of social and economic poverty (although that does clearly exist). Caine has a choice: he can either live like O-Dog, trying to play the gangsta until he's murdered in the street, or he can follow Ronnie (Pinkett) to Atlanta and start a new life away from the violence of Watts. All he has to do is walk away . . .

►

Caine (Turner) is in a dilemma, torn between his violent gang and his good girl, who wants him to change his ways.

Ultimately, Caine's decision results in his death, but the Hughes Brothers present his death as particularly pointless. It could have been prevented at any time, if only Caine had made different choices. That is why, as profoundly disturbing and despairing as the film is, at its core, *Menace II Society* is ultimately a brilliant existentialist tragedy. **MK**

SONATINE 1993 (JAPAN)

Director Takeshi Kitano **Producers** Masayuki Mori, Masayuki Mori, Takio Yoshida
Screenplay Takeshi Kitano **Cinematography** Katsumi Yanagishima **Music** Joe
Hisaishi **Cast** Takeshi Kitano, Aya Kokumai, Tetsu Watanabe, Masanobu Katsumura,
Susumu Terajima, Ren Osugi, Tonbo Zushi, Kenichi Yajima, Eiji Minakata, Kanji Tsuda

As a film describing themes such as "the ephemeral nature of
human existence," it is perhaps appropriate that *Sonatine*
occupies a crucial position within Takeshi Kitano's development
as a director. It is the film in which Kitano's direction reached a
new level of aesthetic and intellectual maturity. *Sonatine*
heralded Kitano's arrival as a visionary filmmaker destined to
become familiar to international audiences. Kitano had long
enjoyed the status of mega-media star in Japan, where his
accomplishments included a successful run as a dynamic
television host, a talented painter and poet, and a comic with
impeccable timing and a penchant for the outrageous.

    Sonatine's plot is deceptively simple, yet it can also be
understood as a culmination of Kitano's talents: it is by turns
violent, and humorous, filled with beautiful compositions and
moments of profound poetic grace. A yakuza mulling over the
possibility of retirement, Aniki Murakawa (Kitano) is sent to
Okinawa with the goal of mediating between two contentious
factions. Murakawa soon learns, however, that his mission is
part of a ruse designed to remove him from Japan so that his
organization can be violently dismantled. Suddenly trapped in

◄

**Director Kitano
plays the lead
in this offbeat
gangster film,
which offers
surprising
moments of
humor and beauty
as relief from the
hard violence.**

an unfamiliar terrain with a steadily decreasing number of men, he retreats to an ocean-side residence. The film then shifts in tone, becoming more meditative and lighthearted, yet with the threat of abrupt violence ever present. Obsessed with Russian roulette and life's transience, Murakawa seems determined to embrace the inevitability of his own destruction, even as the potential for romantic escape in the arms of the

> # "WHEN YOU'RE SCARED ALL THE TIME, YOU REACH A POINT WHEN YOU WISH YOU WERE DEAD." MURAKAWA

alluring Miyuki (Kokumai) lingers as an attractive alternative. Two major motifs dominate the film's second half. The first is Russian roulette (which Kitano plays twice while awake and once in a dream), a game in which the potential for sudden death underscores the role of chance and uncertainty in our lives. It is also, however, a game played voluntarily, revealing an existentialist responsibility on the part of the player. The second motif is the beach as a natural location with transcendental implications. This image is one to which Kitano would return in several of his subsequent films. A more expansive image, it is a sanctuary of sorts, a location where men can be children again and love remains an option. However, that the beach borders the ocean also renders it a symbol of life's transitory and eternal round. It is place of a death and rebirth that will long outlast the petty squabbles of humans with guns. **JM**

► **Murakawa (Kitano) fights for his life in one of the sudden bursts of violence that characterize the movie.**

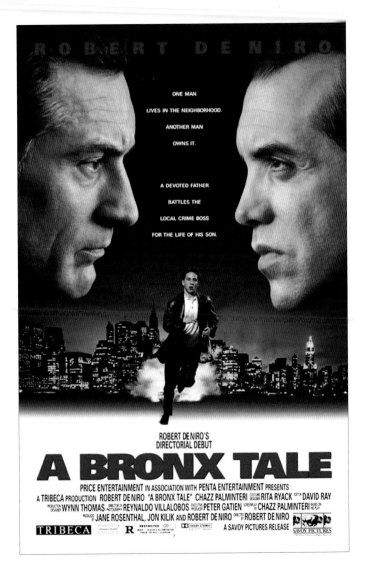

A BRONX TALE 1993 (U.S.)

Director Robert De Niro **Producers** Robert De Niro, Jon Kilik, Jane Rosenthal
Screenplay Chazz Palminteri (from his play) **Cinematography** Reynaldo Villalobos
Music Butch Barbella **Cast** Chazz Palminteri, Robert De Niro, Lillo Brancato, Francis
Capra, Taral Hicks, Kathrine Narducci, Clem Caserta, Joe Pesci, Alfred Sauchelli Jr.

Given Robert De Niro's extraordinary acting career, it may be
considered surprising that it took him as long as it did to
move to the other end of the camera and direct. But unlike
other actors who seem to use their thespian success simply
to leverage themselves into a position of power behind the
camera, De Niro's turns in the director's chair have remained
limited to incidental excursions rather than career revisions.

In this, his directorial debut, De Niro involved himself out
of helpfulness more than anything else. Chazz Palminteri,
then an unknown stage actor, had written and performed a
highly acclaimed one-man show in Los Angeles and Off-
Broadway, drawing some Hollywood attention. Palminteri,
however, refused to sell the rights unless two conditions
were met: he wanted to write the screenplay and play the
key role of mobster Sonny. But since he lacked the right kind
of track record, *A Bronx Tale* remained stage-bound.

Or so it did until De Niro saw the show. Enthralled by
Palminteri's performance and aware of the actor's reluctance
to sell the rights, De Niro agreed to meet Palminteri's
demands, offering to act in it on condition he would direct.

◄
**In his first attempt
at directing, De
Niro delves into
familiar gangster
material, but comes
up with a film
that is held back,
romantic, and
full of subtlety.**

A mere handshake sealed the deal. This story is one of the more charming fairy tales in modern Hollywood history, and the unassuming charm of the resulting production gives it added resonance. For unlike the violent, technically dazzling gangster films De Niro made with Scorsese, *A Bronx Tale* distinguishes itself through its calm, detailed portrayal of a working-class Italian neighborhood in the late 1960s. The

"THE SADDEST THING IN LIFE IS WASTED TALENT."

LORENZO ANELLO

story revolves around Calogero Anello (first Capra, then Brancato), introduced to us in the film at age nine as the son of a bus driver (De Niro) trying to keep his boy on the straight and narrow. The kid's fascination with charismatic mobster Sonny LoSpecchio (an electrifying Palminteri) builds to a crisis when we return to the boy and his battling father figures eight years later.

► **De Niro as director and star manages to get a largely unknown cast to perform wonders in this entertaining portrayal of life in 1960s Bronx.**

Proving himself a true actors' director, De Niro coaxes remarkable performances out of the two boys playing Calogero, showing restraint and subtlety in his admirable handling of an interracial romance. As a gangster film, *A Bronx Tale* may not seek to compete directly with the films in this genre that made De Niro famous. But in its sincere, well-balanced drawing power, *A Bronx Tale* continues to hold its own and attract new admirers. **DHF**

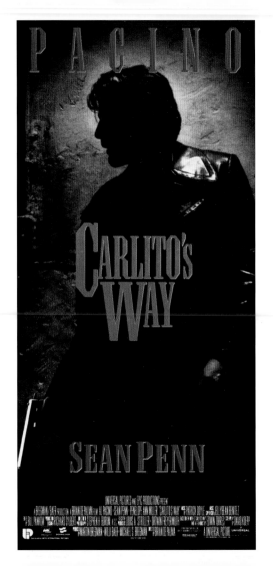

CARLITO'S WAY 1993 (U.S.)

Director Brian De Palma **Producers** Willi Bär, Martin Bregman, Michael Bregman
Screenplay David Koepp **Cinematography** Stephan H. Burum **Music** Patrick
Doyle **Cast** Al Pacino, Sean Penn, Penelope Ann Miller, John Leguizamo, Joseph
Siravo, Viggo Mortensen, Ingrid Rogers, Luis Guzman, James Rebhorn, Jorge Porcel

Brian De Palma's 1993 gangster film is based primarily on the book *After Hours* by New York judge Edwin Torres. Al Pacino stars as Puerto Rican Carlito Brigante, a convicted heroin dealer who, with the help of lawyer Dave Kleinfield (Penn), returns to New York after serving only five years of his thirty-year sentence. Convinced that prison has changed him, Carlito vows to go straight and work toward his quiet dream of running a car-rental business on Paradise Island in the Bahamas. When he reluctantly accompanies his cousin to a poolroom drug deal, a violent shoot-out leaves everyone but Carlito dead. He takes the drug money as a nest egg and begins managing the Paradise Nightclub. There he meets Benny Blanco from the Bronx (Leguizamo)—an up-and-coming drug dealer who covets Carlito's reputation.

Things are looking up for Carlito, but the road to clean living is more difficult than he anticipates. The problems of his coke-addicted lawyer Dave—to whom Carlito owes his freedom—threaten to draw him back under, and despite girlfriend Gail's (Miller) warning to stay away from Dave, Carlito accompanies him as backup when he kills troublesome client

◀
**Although based
on the book *After
Hours*, the movie
was ultimately
named *Carlito's
Way* to avoid
confusion with
Scorsese's movie
After Hours (1985).**

and mobster Vinnie Taglialucci (Siravo). With the mob now after him, Carlito decides to flee with Gail to Florida. At Grand Central Station, he escapes a shoot-out but is then killed on the platform by Blanco.

Despite French critics at *Cahiers du Cinema* naming it one of the best films of the '90s, *Carlito's Way* has never received the (English-language) critical attention and praise it deserves.

"I'VE CHANGED, AND IT DIDN'T TAKE NO THIRTY YEARS LIKE YOUR HONOR THOUGHT, BUT ONLY FIVE." *CARLITO*

The film's flashback structure means that Carlito's fate is revealed in the title sequence, signaling that the crime narrative is really a ruse to enable the film's contemplative, internal focus. Pacino's poetic narration—measured and poignant—is arguably one of the finest ever committed to the screen. It glides and floats with De Palma's steadicam, long shots as they track a reformed man trying desperately to escape to his personal paradise. Carlito's fatal flaw is his sense of loyalty; as critic Matt Zoller Seitz has pointed out, he continually makes the wrong choices for the right reasons.

► **Al Pacino excelled in the part of Carlo Brigante, the drug dealer desperately trying to stay on the straight and narrow.**

The distance between Carlito and the life he wants is amplified by De Palma's voyeuristic camera. As he watches Gail in ballet class from an adjacent rooftop or, most memorably, in a mirror through her latched apartment door, he imagines a life he is ready for, but one he can never fully grasp. **AK**

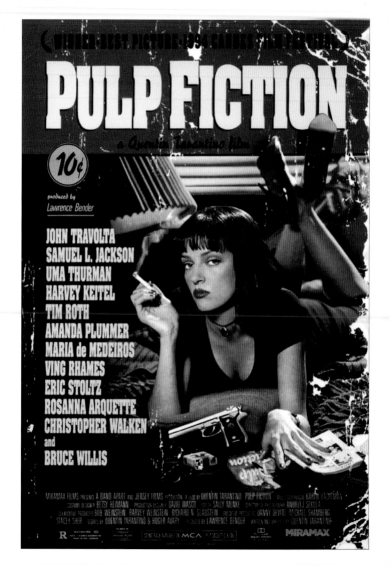

PULP FICTION 1994 (U.S.)

Director Quentin Tarantino **Producer** Lawrence Bender **Screenplay** Quentin
Tarantino, Roger Avary **Cinematography** Andrzej Sekula **Music** Kathy Nelson,
Karyn Rachtman **Cast** John Travolta, Samuel L. Jackson, Tim Roth, Uma Thurman,
Eric Stoltz, Amanda Plummer, Bruce Willis, Maria de Maderios, Rosanna Arquette

If the 1990s can be defined by any single film, for example, like
the 1950s could with *Rebel Without a Cause* (1955), then *Pulp
Fiction* is likely to be the top candidate for such a title. This is
the movie that proved writer/director Quentin Tarantino
wasn't just a one-trick pony after his success with *Reservoir
Dogs* (1992), but was in fact a tremendous auteur, producing
films that could stun viewers.

Pulp Fiction has four intertwining stories: the film starts and
finishes with Pumpkin (Roth) and Honey Bunny (Plummer)
about to rob a coffee shop. Mobsters Vincent Vega (Travolta)
and Jules Winnfield (Jackson) are trying to retrieve a briefcase
owned by their employer Marsellus Wallace (Ving Rhames).
Vega is instructed to take Wallace's young wife, Mia (Thurman),
out for a night on the town. And washed-up boxer Butch
Coolidge (Willis) decides to cross Wallace by not taking a dive
and runs off with the killing he made betting on himself.

The real joy of *Pulp Fiction* is that, although there is a distinct
chronology to these stories—suitcase retrieval, Pumpkin and
Honey Bunny's holdup, the date with Mia, and then Butch's
escape—this is not how the film presents them.

◄

A clever, sassy
movie, *Pulp Fiction*
was awarded
an Oscar for
Best Original
Screenplay,
proving that
Tarantino was
more than just
a one-hit wonder.

Pulp Fiction is infinitely quotable with some terrific, quintessential (Quentinessential?) Tarantino dialogue, but those landmark moments seem to eclipse how tight and consistent that Tarantino-speak is throughout the film. Every character speaks as if they were "QT" himself, and although the director has matured with later pictures, specifically in *Jackie Brown* (1997), where he began to develop more distinct

"HAMBURGERS. THE CORNERSTONE OF ANY NUTRITIOUS BREAKFAST."

JULES WINNFIELD

characterizations, the sheer bravado of two and a half hours of rapid-fire pop culture references is nothing short of exhilarating. The non-stop action that suddenly lurches from humor to violence also makes you gasp.

Tarantino continues what he began in *Reservoir Dogs* in creating a criminal underworld whose logic comes directly from twentieth-century popular culture, the pulp fiction of the '40s and '50s, B movies, and television shows. Unlike the criminal underworld portrayed in *The Godfather* (1972), which purports to have some verisimilitude with reality, Tarantino is not interested in "real" gangsters; he creates his own world where everyone has watched the same movies and read the same books . . . and woe betide any audience member who isn't as clued in to their pop culture as Tarantino, as they're left in the dust while watching the film. **MK**

▶
John Travolta and Samuel L. Jackson played their parts superbly. The movie was a casting triumph.

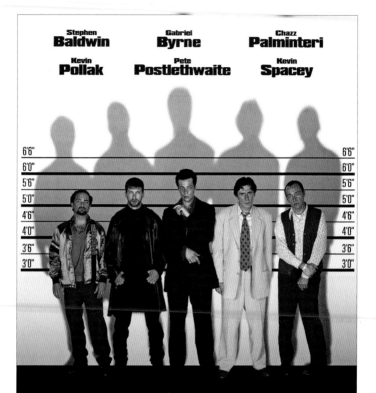

THE USUAL SUSPECTS 1995 (U.S. • GERMANY)

Director Bryan Singer **Producers** Bryan Singer, Michael McDonnell
Screenplay Christopher McQuarrie **Cinematography** Newton Thomas Sigel
Music John Ottman **Cast** Stephen Baldwin, Gabriel Byrne, Benecio Del Toro,
Kevin Pollak, Kevin Spacey, Chazz Palminteri, Pete Postlethwaite, Giancarlo Esposito

From its opening moments, *The Usual Suspects* discloses an arthouse sensibility. This is a crime movie whose story is really about storytelling. Sometimes described as neo-noir, it can also be thought of as a "puzzle" movie—compelling viewers to go back and watch all over again once they've seen how it ends. Exploiting a nonlinear structure, it's told largely in flashback as "Verbal" Kint (Spacey), a con artist and gang member, tells investigator Dave Kujan (Palminteri) about the gang's recent activities. This framing story—Kint sitting in a cop's office—carries an atmospheric sense of enclosure.

Winning an Oscar for best original screenplay, Christopher McQuarrie's script deviously explores a question of identity: who is Keyser Söze? That's what Kujan wants to know, and what Kint might just be able to tell him. Söze is supposedly a "spook story" told by the criminal fraternity, a shadowy figure so clever that he manipulates others like chess pieces, an enigmatic kingpin so all-powerful he can't possibly be real.

Or perhaps "Söze" is really Keaton (Byrne), the leader of Kint's gang, brought together by a police lineup and forming the "usual suspects" of the title. The film plays a few visual tricks to

◀

The original idea behind *The Usual Suspects* stemmed from a title in a magazine, and the iconic poster of the lineup was the first visual template for the movie.

reinforce this possibility, showing us Byrne's reflected face at one point, and lighting him ominously in red immediately after snitch Arturro Marquez (Castula Guerra), has shouted fearfully, "I'm telling you, it's Keyser Söze!"

Jeff Rabin (Dan Hedaya), observes of the office clutter: "All makes sense when you look at it right, you gotta stand back from it." The line is very much a knowing, arthouse conceit

"THE GREATEST TRICK THE DEVIL EVER PULLED WAS CONVINCING THE WORLD HE DIDN'T EXIST." *"VERBAL" KINT*

buried in a genre tale, a wink at the audience that there's more going on in the story-behind-the-story. John Ottman's slick editing and Singer's direction contribute greatly to the film's punch line, showing Kujan's epiphany via a slow-mo dropped, shattered coffee mug, and ending on a brilliantly timed shot of black nothingness over just a few words of dialogue.

Like investigator Kujan, we have to stand back. Söze appears on-screen as an iconic gangster, all flowing coat and hat, deftly flicking a lighter and sharply leveling a gun. He's what gangsters are supposed to look like; he's a glamorized, mythicized version of what we expect to see. But the iconography of film genre can deceive. The lesson of *The Usual Suspects*, carried in one bravura shot of a character simply walking down the street, is that we shouldn't judge by appearances, or by genre clichés. Suddenly, just like that, our certainties can be gone. **MH**

► Kevin Spacey in
The Usual Suspects:
a film that delights
in playing tricks
on its audience.

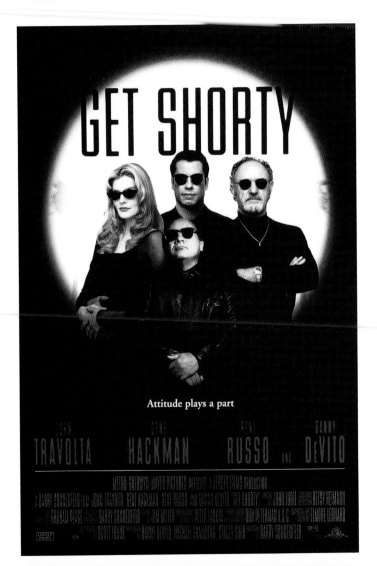

GET SHORTY 1995 (U.S.)

Director Barry Sonnenfeld **Producers** Danny DeVito, Barry Sonnenfeld, Michael Shamberg, Stacey Sher **Screenplay** Scott Frank (based on the Elmore Leonard novel) **Cinematography** Donald Peterman **Music** John Lurie **Cast** John Travolta, Gene Hackman, Rene Russo, Danny DeVito, Dennis Farina, Delroy Lindo, Jon Gries

Fresh off his renaissance role as Vincent Vega in Quentin Tarantino's *Pulp Fiction* (1994), John Travolta continued one of the most impressive comebacks in La-la-land history with a different brand of hip mobster as Chili Palmer in this Barry Sonnenfeld–helmed adaptation of the 1990 Elmore Leonard tome. A gangster film where style trumps substance, *Get Shorty* rams the ego-driven worlds of Hollywood and organized crime into each other in a meta-cool feast of clothes, stars, and attitude.

Travolta does style with the best, and this film is a great example. Walking up the stairs of a swank bistro to a meeting with schlockmeister Harry Zimm (Hackman), Travolta's über-confident carriage is reminiscent of his classic opening swagger-stroll in *Saturday Night Fever* (1977). His charisma is the driving force that propels Chili from Miami loansharking with rival Ray "Bones" Barboni (Farina) to Hollywood deal-making with mega-star Martin Weir (DeVito, who also produced for his Jersey Films)—the titular "get" target. Along the way he does some fighting (Lindo and the pre-*Sopranos* Gandolfini) and, of course, does some loving—Rene Russo as

◀

Having been the cameraman for one somber gangster movie (*Miller's Crossing*), director Barry Sonnenfeld delivers a cracking, wisecracking comedy of manners in this movie.

B-film scream queen Karen Flores, who just happens to be Shorty's ex and Zimm's current. The key conceit of the film is that the denizens of the criminal underworld and those of the cinematic glamour world operate in eerily similar ways. But Chili, a major film buff who fits right in with Tinseltown's duplicitous milieu, has an ace up his designer-suit sleeve: the occasional application of a tasteful dose of muscle. He

"IF YOU'RE GONNA SET SOMEBODY UP, IT'S GOTTA BE A SURPRISE, YOU GOT THAT?" CHILI PALMER

demonstrates that an abundance of cool can serve a motivated person quite well in the land where poseurs rule. The beautiful people listen when he tells them, "I'm the guy who's telling you the way it is."

Get Shorty reverberates with original, gritty, profane, often hilarious dialogue, a wonderful jazz-inflected score by John Lurie, and action that flows swiftly from set piece to set piece. In the end, though, it is not much more than an entertaining, star-powered diversion. It navigates the same streets, restaurants, and back lots as Robert Altman's The Player (1992), but its near-contemporary leaves the viewer with a much more sinister aftertaste. For all the thugs and thug wannabes on display, Get Shorty is gangster-lite. It throws a few punches, and not more than one person even gets killed. But what it really wants to do is direct—or at least produce. **WSW**

► John Travolta is the comeback kid, riding on the crest of another gangster movie following Pulp Fiction with even more snappy dialogue and suits.

Robert
DE NIRO

Sharon
STONE

Joe
PESCI

NO ONE

STAYS

AT THE

TOP

FOREVER.

A MARTIN SCORSESE PICTURE

CASINO

UNIVERSAL PICTURES AND SYALIS D.A. & LEGENDE ENTREPRISES PRESENT A DE FINA/CAPPA PRODUCTION

A MARTIN SCORSESE PICTURE "CASINO" DON RICKLES KEVIN POLLAK JAMES WOODS

COSTUME DESIGNERS RITA RYACK JOHN DUNN EDITOR THELMA SCHOONMAKER PRODUCTION DESIGNED BY DANTE FERRETTI

DIRECTOR OF PHOTOGRAPHY ROBERT RICHARDSON A.S.C. BASED ON THE BOOK BY NICHOLAS PILEGGI SCREENPLAY BY NICHOLAS PILEGGI & MARTIN SCORSESE

PRODUCED BY BARBARA DE FINA DIRECTED BY MARTIN SCORSESE A UNIVERSAL PICTURE

CASINO 1995 (U.S. • FRANCE)

Director Martin Scorsese **Producer** Babara De Fina **Screenplay** Nicholas Pileggi, Martin Scorsese **Cinematography** Robert Richardson **Music** Bobby Mackston
Cast Robert De Niro, Sharon Stone, Joe Pesci, James Woods, Frank Vincent, Pasquale Cajano, Kevin Pollak, Don Rickles, Vinny Vella, Alan King, L. Q. Jones, Dick Smothers

At the center of *Casino*'s exuberant narrative is Sam "Ace" Rothstein (De Niro), a Mob-connected professional gambler who is given the job of running the Tangiers casino in Las Vegas for the Mob's Chicago outfit. He is joined here by his childhood friend, the violent and unpredictable Nicky Santoro (Pesci), who arrives in town hoping to get his own taste of the Vegas sweet life. Times are good, and one night at the Tangiers Ace meets hustler Ginger (Stone). Despite her initial protestations and his better judgment, they marry and move into an ostentatious trophy home.

Before long things begin to spiral out of control; Nicky is banned from Las Vegas casinos for his hustling and begins systematized burglaries to make money. Ace also realizes that Ginger, now an alcoholic and cocaine addict, cannot break ties with her lecherous ex-boyfriend Lester Diamond (Woods), whom she is giving money and making plans to run off with. Things at the Tangiers go from bad to worse when the FBI seizes the casino and goes through the books, prompting an unrivaled spree of violence where the Chicago outfit kill everyone who could potentially incriminate them. As part of

◄
Scorsese's 1970s Mob tale–cum–"urban western" came in just over three hours long, and was shot in Las Vegas over 100 days. Joe Pesci reprised his psychopath role from *Goodfellas*.

this rampage, the bosses beat Nicky and bury him alive in the desert. In the opening sequence of the film, which sits at the tail end of the plot, Ace is nearly killed by a car bomb—though we're never sure who planted it.

Scorsese's film is, above all, an exercise in cinematic excess. The mise-en-scène constructs a Las Vegas more brilliant and excessive than any picture before or since: from Rothstein's

"CASINO MAY BE HIS (SCORSESE'S) ULTIMATE EXPERIMENT IN BROKEN FILM." *GAVIN SMITH*

over-coordinated pastel suits to the interiors of the casino itself, each detail is as polished and reflective as Ginger's diamond jewelry. Part of this functions as a critique of materialism, but more than this, *Casino* is Scorsese's epic testament to his obsession with the cinematic medium. From the moment the film begins, its narrators open fire on the spectator with narrative detail, overloading the plot with dizzying numbers of characters and shifting allegiances. Through this, and the camera's flamboyant gesturing, *Casino* becomes so busy and gaudy that, at some point, the world of the movie shatters like a glass chandelier falling to the floor—a spectacular explosion of glass, light, and violence that manifests through both narrative and form. Although many critics initially found the film indulgent and problematic, *Casino* has matured into a classic of the genre. **AK**

► Sharon Stone was a revelation as De Niro's sassy, gold-digging wife, Ginger—a role for which she was nominated for an Oscar.

HEAT 1995 (U.S.)

Director Michael Mann **Producers** Michael Mann, Art Linson **Screenplay** Michael Mann **Cinematography** Dante Spinotti **Music** Elliot Goldenthal **Cast** Al Pacino, Robert De Niro, Val Kilmer, Tom Sizemore, Ashley Judd, Jon Voight, Amy Brenneman, Danny Trejo, Diane Venora, Mykelti Williamson, Wes Studi, Dennis Haysbert

Director Michael Mann has long been acknowledged as a master of the modern police procedural. From the television series, and later film, *Miami Vice* (1984, 2006), through *Thief* (1981), *Manhunter* (1986), and *Collateral* (2004), Mann has created that uniquely contemporary crime drama that melds high stylization with a gritty social outlook. *Heat* is perhaps Mann's peak achievement in the genre, a slick, cynical cops-and-robbers drama front-loaded with those two sacred monsters of acting, Al Pacino and Robert De Niro.

De Niro portrays career thief Neil McCauley heading a team of high-end thieves who, after a fatal armored car robbery, hope to pull off one last big bank job before retiring. Pacino plays Vincent Hanna, a grizzled homicide detective tracking Neil's crew with a team of his own.

It has been said that Pacino and De Niro never actually appear in-frame together, and this makes sense, as their characters are in some ways the same man. It would be like Dr. Jekyll and Mr. Hyde appearing together, although Hanna and McCauley are closer in kind than this. They are on opposite sides of the law, but the same side of life, career men wizened

◀

Teaming up De Niro with Pacino and Mann for the first time should have spelled box office success. The outcome is a touch disappointing.

by the grim realities of their jobs, which just happen to coincide, and their mutually doomed personal lives. The film is a kind of cat-and-mouse love story between two men who have equal parts contempt and respect for each other. Their relationships with women, and, in Hanna's case, a daughter, are sacrificed to their over driven commitment to their jobs. McCauley states his code explicitly: "Never have anything in your life that you can't

"NEVER HAVE ANYTHING IN YOUR LIFE THAT YOU CAN'T WALK OUT ON."

NEIL MCCAULEY

walk out on in thirty seconds flat if you spot the heat coming around the corner," a belief system that, when challenged, makes for one of the film's most devastating moments.

Heat is as textural as it is visceral. Mann's notorious attention to details (background light-blurs, a car's color) renders Los Angeles as a dense layered presence, which, for all its lights and energy, remains coolly abstract. The high-powered shoot-outs and chase scenes are particularly authentic, as well-known actors, six months into production, look like twenty-year veterans. The disrupted bank heist is masterfully staged and edited, with the sunny streets of L.A. erupting in an orchestrated mayhem of gunfire, bullet-riddled cars, and bewildered bystanders. The film ends with a classic shoot-out between the two leads on the fields of L.A.'s airport, where it's clear that one of them has to die. Watch it and see which one. **GC**

► **Detective Vincent Hanna is played by Al Pacino, who will always resonate with gangster movie audiences.**

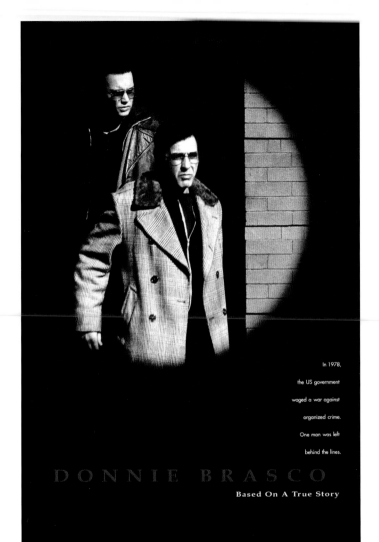

In 1978,

the US government

waged a war against

organized crime.

One man was left

behind the lines.

DONNIE BRASCO

Based On A True Story

DONNIE BRASCO 1997 (U.S.)

Director Mike Newell **Producers** Louis DiGiaimo, Mark Johnson, Barry Levinson, Gail Mutrux **Screenplay** Paul Attanasio (from the book by Joseph D. Pistone and Richard Woodley) **Cinematography** Peter Sova **Music** Patrick Doyle **Cast** Johnny Depp, Al Pacino, Michael Madsen, Bruno Kirby, James Russo, Anne Heche, Rocco Sisto

Donnie Brasco is an undercover cop story based on true events. Those "events" are so shrouded in "code" language, however, so shady, ambiguous, and disputed, that instead of focusing on action the film only looks at its protagonists—they, instead of their actions, are the key to the story.

Fittingly, most of the time in *Donnie Brasco* we watch mobsters shuffling around, doing absolutely nothing except fantasize about their "big break." Among those gangsters are Benjamin "Lefty" Rugiero (Pacino), Sonny Black (Madsen), and Donnie Brasco (Depp). Donnie is in reality Joe Pistone, an undercover agent from the FBI. He befriends Lefty, whose low ranking in the mob and family problems make him vulnerable and desperate. For Donnie, Lefty is a way into the "family." For Lefty, Donnie is a way to finally get up and ahead (parallels between the Mafia's hierarchy and social stratification are pressed throughout the movie). Before long the two become real friends. When Sonny is "promoted" to run the borough of Brooklyn and tries to become more independent, the stakes are raised. Donnie then knows he will eventually betray Lefty's friendship. It pains him so much that he drifts away from his

◄

Al Pacino gives one of his best performances— and that's saying something for an actor who has given us a host of memorable cops and villains—as a small-time crook under suspicion from the cops.

own family. When Donnie and Lefty are ordered to execute someone, the cover is finally lifted. Lefty is "sent for"; he will be assassinated. Donnie is decorated and "comes home."

It is to *Donnie Brasco's* advantage that director Mike Newell is not a gangster movie specialist. Newell's direction allows Pacino and Depp to explore the emotional nuances of their characters to the fullest. Lefty's role as a "spoke in a wheel," as

"A WISEGUY'S ALWAYS RIGHT. EVEN WHEN HE'S WRONG HE'S RIGHT."

BENJAMIN "LEFTY" RUGGIERO

he calls, it, is one of Pacino's most impressive performances, restrained and compassionate. Depp's Donnie, meanwhile, is an acting tour de force. His slide away from his family into Lefty's is portrayed so subtly that it is almost unnoticeable.

Like Lefty, *Donnie Brasco* is often overlooked in the gangster genre, probably because the film does not mythologize gangsters. Rather, it tries to show them as part of the same rat race to get ahead that everyone else in the world is part of. Nor does the film glorify the upholders of the law. The FBI's treatment of Donnie is as cold-hearted as the Mafia's attitude toward Lefty, and Donnie himself feels increasingly disgusted with his job. Exactly because it shows those many shades of gray, and because it introduced the world to the catchphrase "badabing, badaboom," *Donnie Brasco* deserves its place in the pantheon of gangster cinema. **EM**

►
Al Pacino as Lefty instructs undercover cop (Depp) in his riveting portrayal of Donnie Brasco.

L.A. CONFIDENTIAL 1997 (U.S.)

Director Curtis Hanson **Producers** Curtis Hanson, Arnold Milchan, Michael G. Nathanson **Screenplay** Brian Helgeland, Curtis Hanson (from the novel by James Ellroy) **Cinematography** Dante Spinotti **Music** Jerry Goldsmith **Cast** Russell Crowe, Guy Pearce, Kevin Spacey, Kim Basinger, Danny DeVito, James Cromwell

What a travesty the Oscars were in 1998: *Titanic* swept the board so thoroughly that a film as nuanced, detailed, complicated, and grown-up as *L.A. Confidential* barely got a look in. In any other year, Curtis Hanson's picture would definitely have been the one to beat.

Based on the novel by James Ellroy, *L.A. Confidential* weaves together several seemingly unrelated narrative strands all focusing on the corruption in the L.A.P.D. in the early 1950s. Jack Vincennes (Spacey) is a flashy cop who has been hired as "technical adviser" for a TV show called *Badge of Honor* (loosely based on *Dragnet*), and who enjoys his Hollywood friends and influence more than actually doing his job in law enforcement. Bud White (Crowe) is a brooding powerhouse of a cop, perhaps lacking in higher reasoning skills, but dedicated to the job. Ed Exley (Pearce) is a by-the-book, college-educated officer who has much to learn about the realities of policework. Lynne Bracken (Basinger) is the clichéd whore with a heart of gold who bears an uncanny resemblance to Veronica Lake, and who becomes romantically involved with Officer White. Finally, Sig Hudgens

◄

The 1940s noir-style poster says it all: sex, glamor, and crime in this corruption drama with plenty of twists and turns.

(DeVito) is a sleazy tabloid reporter who is Vincennes' key contact to the world of Hollywood sleaze. What draws all five of these characters together is a massacre in an all-night café, dubbed by the press the "Nite Owl Massacre," named after the location itself, and what investigating this atrocity reveals is the extent of the corruption in the police force and an elite prostitution ring that offers its clients movie-star

> ## "OH, GREAT. YOU GET THE GIRL, I GET THE CORONER."
>
> *JACK VINCENNES*

look-alike call girls—including White's girl, Bracken. Like the classic noirs of old, *L.A. Confidential*'s plot is dizzyingly labyrinthine, much like Howard Hawks' *The Big Sleep* (1946). The murder mystery itself, the question of who is responsible for the Nite Owl Massacre, is the impetus for the film's exploration of the police force's corruption. What gets evoked through this is a story about the ambiguities of justice, of whether or not police officers can be "above the law" in bringing bad guys to justice. And, in typical Ellroy style, the film poses the question of what happens when the bad guys turn out to be the good guys, and the good guys are actually the bad guys.

As the pick of a perfect cast, Kim Basinger won an Oscar for her portrayal of the Veronica Lake lookalike—subtle, startling, alluring, and immensely assured. **MK**

► Warring cops battle it out, including Russell Crowe and Guy Pearce giving finely judged performances.

LOCK, STOCK AND TWO SMOKING BARRELS 1998 (U.K.)

Director Guy Ritchie **Producer** Matthew Vaughn **Screenplay** Guy Ritchie
Cinematography Tim Maurice-Jones **Music** David A. Hughes, John Murphy
Cast Jason Flemyng, Dexter Fletcher, Nick Moran, Jason Statham, Steven Mackintosh,
Nicholas Rowe, Nick Marcq, Charles Forbes, Vinnie Jones, Lenny McLean

Quentin Tarantino's influence on the film industry in the 1990s
is hard to exaggerate: not only did the critical success of
Reservoir Dogs (1992) and the cultural phenomenon of *Pulp
Fiction* (1994) inspire a seemingly endless spate of "hipster
thrillers" that thrived on relentless violence and self-reflexive
dialogue, but the cult of celebrity that came to surround
Tarantino as a self-made writer-director ushered in a generation
of independent filmmakers who sought to catapult themselves
to instant fame by producing a low-budget debut to serve as a
calling card for Hollywood.

Guy Ritchie may be seen as a prime example of this trend. His
first film, *Lock, Stock and Two Smoking Barrels* was shot on 16mm
with a shoestring budget, but Ritchie's grander aspirations are
made clear through his use of high-profile celebrity cameos
and the genuine media savvy with which the film was launched
in the U.K. as a strongly hyped "next big thing." Ritchie's
confidence as a first-time director is indeed impressive, as he
brings a great deal of style and panache to a screenplay that

◀

**Director Guy
Ritchie managed
to make a name
for himself with
his stylish *Lock,
Stock and Two
Smoking Barrels*.**

seems hell-bent on careening all over the place until the proverbial wheels come off. Bolstered by a soundtrack full of high-octane pop music and the rough appeal of its cast of then-unknowns, the film's editing gives this comedic caper plenty of pace, and succeeds in being entertaining even when its labyrinthine plot becomes all but impossible to follow. But as continuous self-reflexive jabs and twists remind us all the

"THERE'S NO MONEY, THERE'S NO WEED. IT'S ALL BEEN REPLACED BY A PILE OF CORPSES." TOM

time, the intricacies of the story are of hardly more importance than the wafer-thin character sketches, for this is an exercise in style over substance. The same thing could be said about Ritchie's follow-up picture, the more sophisticated but otherwise similar *Snatch* (2000), and Ritchie's subsequent career seems to confirm his status as a one-trick pony. Ritchie has explored other genres and styles, but has had any degree of success only when revisiting similar themes.

> ►
> **Combining little-known actors with smashing one-liners and equally hard-hitting action and violence, the movie struck gold with audiences.**

Besides this low-budget debut, perhaps Ritchie's most lasting contribution to film history will be his discovery of Jason Statham, the former athlete and model who developed into a leading man in a specific brand of action films. After this debut, Statham drew on his martial arts background and everyman tough-guy persona in a string of action hits, from *The Transporter* (2002) to *Crank* (2006) and *Death Race* (2008). **DHF**

SEXY BEAST 2001 (U.K. • SPAIN)

Director Jonathan Glazer **Producer** Jeremy Thomas **Screenplay** Louis Mellis, David Scinto **Cinematography** Ivan Bird **Music** Roque Baños **Cast** Ray Winstone, Ben Kingsley, Ian McShane, Amanda Redman, James Fox, Cavan Kendall, Julianne White, Álvaro Monje, Robert Atiko, Nieves del Amo Oruet, Enrique Alemán Fabrega

When a film opens on a bronzed Ray Winstone, replete with skimpy skin-tight Speedos, you know you are in for something entirely different. The normally gruffly charming Winstone plays Gary "Gal" Dove, an ex-London gangster trying to lead a sedate life of "retirement" in an idyllic Spanish villa with his wife, Deedee (Redman), having turned his back on his former life of crime. That is until his former boss sends out crazed enforcer Don Logan (Kingsley) to recruit him for one last job and provide a little bit of "gentle" persuasion. Jack Carter's (played by Michael Caine) observation in *Get Carter* that he was "a big man but out of shape" was never more accurate than here, as Winstone plays against type in portraying Gal as a meek, weak-willed man trying desperately to hide from his past while quietly enjoying the fruits of his former career. In a brilliant piece of counter-casting, Winstone—so often the enforcer himself—comes across as a gentle and cuddlesome man trying to forge a new life but shackled to his past.

It's Logan's arrival that sends Gal's sedate existence haywire as the unexpected visitor makes himself the most unwelcome of houseguests after his initial requests for Gal to help out his

◄
Ray Winstone was given the choice of playing Gal or Don; he opted for the out-of-character part of Gal, giving Kingsley the chance to win an Oscar.

old boss turns into a stream of increasingly threatening vitriol. Ben Kingsley's Logan, a character as far removed from his earlier portrayal of Gandhi as you could possibly imagine, steals the show and garnered an Oscar nomination for Best Supporting Actor. His acerbic and intense performance is at the heart of *Sexy Beast*'s success; the energy he brings to the acting is in direct contrast to the sleepy impression of Gal.

"IT'S NOT WHAT YOU'RE SAYING. IT'S ALL THIS STUFF YOU'RE NOT SAYING. INSINNUENDOS." *DON LOGAN*

Kingsley manages to infuse him with such chilling menace that long after the final frame has run, you're sure to remember Don Logan, the character of which Kingsley claims was based largely on his grandmother.

Part of a rash of Brit-gangster flicks at the turn of the millennium, *Sexy Beast* sets itself apart as a character study of a man trying to break from his past but who is still tortured by the ghosts of who and what he used to be. As the debut feature by former advertising director Jonathan Glazer, the picture is lively and packed with surprises, playing out as part Mob film and partly the darkest of dark comedies, with surreal episodes thrown in. The job itself is a Hitchcockian McGuffin—the real drama is in the battle of wills between Gal's past in the shape of the fearful Logan, and his future in the shape of his wife, Deedee. **RH**

► A menacing-looking Ben Kingsley pulls out all the stops to create crazed mobster Don Logan—a far cry from his famous Gandhi role.

ROAD TO PERDITION 2002 (U.S.)

Director Sam Mendes **Producers** Sam Mendes, Dean Zanuck, Richard D. Zanuck
Screenplay David Self (based on the eponymous graphic novel inspired by
the *Lone Wolf and Cub* manga) **Cinematography** Conrad L. Hall **Music** Thomas
Newman **Cast** Tom Hanks, Tyler Hoechlin, Paul Newman, Stanley Tucci, Jude Law

Sam Mendes' follow-up to his much lauded and Oscar-winning
film *American Beauty* (1999) was a distinct change of pace,
although there is no doubt he could have had his pick of
A-list pictures, he instead went for this odd period piece of a
gangster film based partly on a *Lone Wolf and Cub*–inspired
graphic novel by Max Allan Collins and Richard Piers Rayner,
and partly on actual events involving a traitorous enforcer for
real-life mobster John Looney.

In 1931, young Michael Sullivan Jr. (Hoechlin) inadvertently
discovers what his father (Hanks) does for a living—he's a
trusted enforcer for the notorious John Rooney (Newman),
who in turn is protected by Capone's enforcer, Frank Nitti
(Tucci). Sullivan Sr. has been very careful about shielding his
family from the reality of his job, but when his elder son
accidentally witnesses the murder of another mobster, he
must choose between his family and his mob. Rooney's
morally weak son, Conner (Craig), is worried that Michael Jr.
doesn't know enough to keep quiet, and orders a hit on the
Sullivan household, killing Sullivan's wife (Leigh) and younger
boy. With only father and son remaining and on the run, the

◀

The dark, shadowy
poster design
not only reflects
the brooding
atmosphere of
Road to Perdition,
but also gives
a hint of the
graphic novel
behind the movie.

two try to find a way to stop Conner and fight back against the mob. *Road to Perdition* so wants to be *The Godfather* (1972) you can taste it. Like Coppola's film, what should have been a well-produced B movie is given the full prestige makeover. It's a very pretty film, immaculate even, but it never wholly rises above its pulp literary antecedents. Conard Hall's Oscar-winning cinematography not only photographs beautiful

"THIS IS SUPREMELY CRAFTED, GROWN-UP MOVIEMAKING THAT NEVER ESCAPES ITS PULP ORIGINS." IAN NATHAN

images, but also captures the compositions and framing of the underlying graphic novel. Hall and Mendes sought to give their picture the look of the works of artist Edward Hopper, and have largely succeeded.

The film also provides insight into the Irish mob of the early 1930s and its connections with Capone's organization, exemplified by the role of Frank Nitti's position in trying to broker a treaty between Rooney and Sullivan. This is a very different presentation of Nitti than one sees in most gangster movies—Tucci is certainly not Billy Drago in *The Untouchables* (1987)—and is probably more like the historical enforcer than other depictions. This Nitti is much more like a senior vice president than a mobster, and by 1931, was probably quite close to Nitti's day-to-day job than gunning down the opposition on Chicago streets. **MK**

► A visual treat, *Road to Perdition* deservedly won the Oscar for Best Cinematography.

criminal employers of the police's plans and Chen does his best to keep his superior officers secretly apprised of his gang's plans. When SP Wong Chi Shing (Wong), the only officer who knows Chen's true allegiance, is killed in a spectacular fashion, the picture takes a sudden turn that sends Chen and Lau on a collision course. *Infernal Affairs* was remade in 2006 by Martin Scorsese as the Academy Award–winning film *The Departed*.

"IF YOU SEE SOMEONE DOING SOMETHING BUT AT THE SAME TIME WATCHING YOU THEN HE IS A COP." *KEUNG*

His interpretation of Lau and Mak's film lacks some of the crucial nuances that makes *Infernal Affairs* so compelling. In particular, the moles in Scorsese's adaptation, played by Leonardo DiCaprio and Matt Damon, are not as complex as their Hong Kong predecessors, Chen and Lau. *Infernal Affairs*, though an intricate and action-packed crime thriller, is essentially a character study concerned with deconstructing the categories of "good" and "bad." Chen, though ultimately determined to rejoin the police force after he has sufficiently foiled the Triad's illegal activities, is occasionally enticed by the illicit allure of the gangster, whereas Lau, initially a "mob informer," actively desires to become an officer of the law. Such intricacy contributed to *Infernal Affairs'* success, allowing Lau and Mak to helm follow-up features, *Infernal Affairs II* (2003), a prequel, and *Infernal Affairs III* (2003), which is at once a sequel *and* a prequel. **AKu**

► Supt Wong (played by Anthony Wong) feels the heat as the Triads move in.

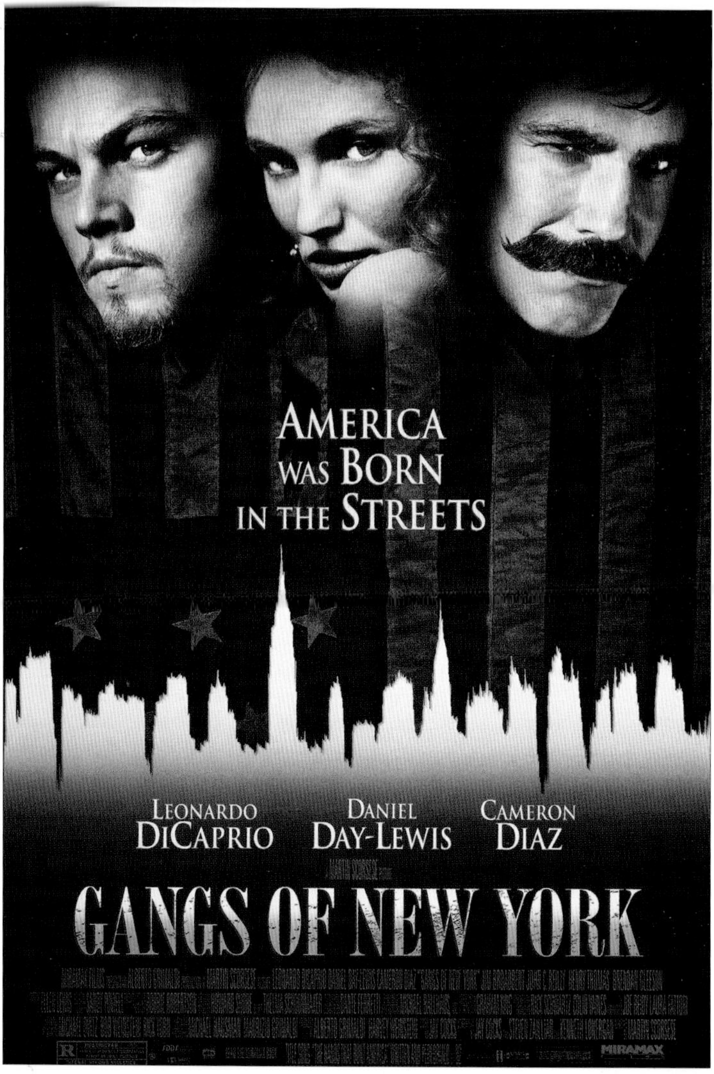
AMERICA
WAS BORN
IN THE STREETS
LEONARDO DICAPRIO
DANIEL DAY-LEWIS
CAMERON DIAZ
GANGS OF NEW YORK
MIRAMAX

GANGS OF NEW YORK 2002 (U.S.)

Director Martin Scorsese **Producers** Alberto Grimaldi, Harvey Weinstein
Screenplay Jay Cocks, Steven Zaillian, Kenneth Lonergan (story by Jack Cocks)
Cinematography Michael Ballhaus **Music** Howard Shore **Cast** Leonardo DiCaprio,
Daniel Day-Lewis, Cameron Diaz, Jim Broadbent, John C. Reilly, Liam Neeson

Characteristically laden with themes of Mob loyalty, religious
conflict, and violent retributions, Martin Scorsese's tale of mid-
nineteenth-century gangland New York presents a ruthless and
decadent collection of killers, thieves, noblemen, and peasants.
Boatloads of immigrant arrivals face brutal resistance, racial and
cultural tensions spill over, and gang members roam the streets
intent on exerting their supremacy and guarding their territory.

   Pivotal to this social disorder, and to the atmosphere of
violence, is the villainous Bill "The Butcher" Cutting (Day-Lewis),
who wields a ruthless authority over the occupants of the blood-
soaked streets. Perceiving himself as the true Native American,
the reactionary Butcher is the figurehead of a pervading trend
toward close-minded Protestant American patriotism and
revulsion at the perceived invasion.

   The bloody and spectacular opening battle scene, in which
the Butcher slays Irish gang leader Priest Vallon (Neeson), is
choreographed in unison with a pounding score, and sets an
overtly dramatic tone for the rest of the picture. As in so many of
Scorsese's films, characters like the Butcher and the Priest
embody a striking juxtaposition of religion and violence, typical

◄

**The movie had
been considered
Scorsese's grand
folly because
he had been so
obsessed with the
idea for so long,
but it proved to
be a historical epic.**

of such lawless times. Emphasizing the inherent hypocrisies in gang life, Scorsese reveals how fierce loyalty and adherence to moral codes can coincide with bloodshed.

Having witnessed the killing of his father as a young boy, the Priest's now fully grown son Amsterdam Vallon (DiCaprio) anonymously returns to New York several years later, determined to make a better life for himself. However, given the scope of the

"I'M 47. 47 YEARS OLD. YOU KNOW HOW I STAYED ALIVE THIS LONG? FEAR."

BILL "THE BUTCHER" CUTTING

Butcher's domination, Amsterdam is inevitably assimilated into the Butcher's circle and ultimately taken under his fatherly wing. Ensuing scenes recall the symbolic resonance of the early father-and-son scene between Priest and the young Amsterdam (in particular the Priest's ritualistic practice that "the blood stays on the razor"). But paternal sentimentality turns out to be the Butcher's weakness: "I never had a son," he says in rueful mood, unaware that Amsterdam is all the while plotting his revenge.

▶ Daniel Day-Lewis gives a towering performance as the aptly named Bill "The Butcher" Cutting, who has a penchant for throwing knives.

Although it was not the film that ultimately gained Scorsese his long-overdue Oscar (he had to wait until *The Departed* [2006] to receive that honor), *Gangs of New York* remains a triumph, and reminiscent of Scorsese's earlier *Goodfellas* (1990) in its power to capture the internal politics, plotting, and multi-layered deceptions of gangster life. It is one of the crowning achievements of his later output. **SR**

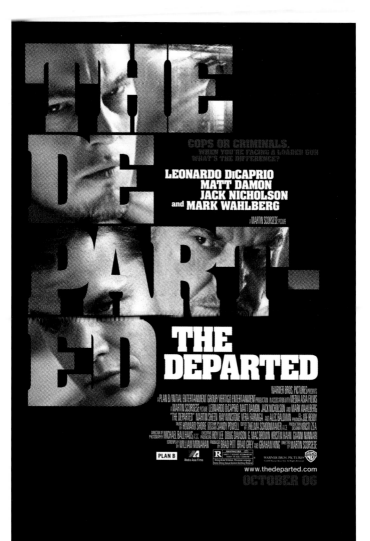

THE DEPARTED 2006 (U.S. • HONG KONG)

Director Martin Scorsese **Producers** Brad Grey, Graham King, Gianni Nunnari, Brad Pitt **Screenplay** William Monahan (based on the screenplay by Siu Fai Mak and Felix Chong) **Cinematography** Michael Ballhaus **Music** Howard Shore **Cast** Leonardo DiCaprio, Matt Damon, Jack Nicholson, Mark Wahlberg, Martin Sheen

Based upon the internationally successful Hong Kong action film *Infernal Affairs* (2002) and its two sequels (*Infernal Affairs II* and *Infernal Affairs III*, both 2003), Martin Scorsese's *The Departed* received both popular and critical acclaim, winning four Academy Awards, including Best Picture, Best Director, and Best Adapted Screenplay. Celebrated by many as a return to the gritty crime dramas largely responsible for Scorsese's emergence as one of world cinema's most exciting and daring talents, *The Departed* features strong performances from Matt Damon and Leonardo DiCaprio as "moles" working undercover for the mob and the police respectively. Furthermore, while it ultimately falls short of the dauntingly high bar set by masterpieces like 1976's *Taxi Driver*, 1980's *Raging Bull*, and 1990's *Goodfellas*, *The Departed*'s action unfolds at a steady pace, propelled along by plenty of the director's trademark stylistic flourishes, from the skillful manipulation of the film's soundtrack to an array of dizzying whip-pans and complex tracking shots.

Scorsese and screenwriter William Monahan make several crucial changes in adapting the *Infernal Affairs* films for Western, primarily North American, audiences. Nevertheless, they

◄

Was it a consolation Oscar that Martin Scorsese finally bagged with this rework of the hard-to-beat original *Infernal Affairs*?

endeavor to retain *Infernal Affairs'* themes of deception and conflicted loyalties, as well as several of the remarkable set pieces that made the *Infernal Affairs* series so appealing. Perhaps the most visually arresting of these adapted sequences would be the startlingly violent elevator scene, which loses none of its dramatic power or shock potential in the process of translation. More difficult—and perhaps most striking because of its

"COPS, OR CRIMINALS . . . WHEN YOU'RE FACING A LOADED GUN, WHAT'S THE DIFFERENCE?" *FRANK COSTELLO*

ultimate success—is the transplantation of the narrative's action from the glossy post-modern cityscape of contemporary Hong Kong to the grimy, violent, economically depressed suburbs south of Boston, Massachusetts. By engaging directly with the myriad racial, ethnic, and political tensions that have defined the volatile New England city for decades, Scorsese and Monahan transform what could have easily been yet another simple but effective remake into a serious and culturally specific engagement with shifting conceptions of masculinity, ethnicity, and gender at the dawn of the new millennium. The Irish Americans on either side of *The Departed*'s precariously "thin blue line" are every bit as fully realized as the Italian Americans featured prominently in Scorsese's 1973 film, *Mean Streets*. In this sense, *The Departed* advances tropes that have long informed Scorsese's oeuvre. **JM**

► Colin (Damon) plays a deadly game of hide-and-seek after realizing he is being followed in Chinatown.

FROM ACCLAIMED DIRECTOR DAVID CRONENBERG

EVERY SIN LEAVES A MARK.

VIGGO MORTENSEN   NAOMI WATTS   VINCENT CASSEL

EASTERN PROMISES

FOCUS FEATURES PRESENTS IN ASSOCIATION WITH BBC FILMS & KUDOS PICTURES/SERENDIPITY POINT FILMS PRODUCTION IN ASSOCIATION WITH SCION FILMS A FILM BY DAVID CRONENBERG VIGGO MORTENSEN NAOMI WATTS VINCENT CASSEL "EASTERN PROMISES" ARMIN MUELLER-STAHL CASTING DEIRDRE BOWEN, NINA GOLD MUSIC BY HOWARD SHORE EDITOR DENISE CRONENBERG EDITOR RONALD SANDERS DESIGNER CAROL SPIER DIRECTOR OF PHOTOGRAPHY PETER SUSCHITZKY PRODUCERS TRACEY SEAWARD EXECUTIVE PRODUCERS STEPHEN GARRETT, DAVID M. THOMPSON, JEFF ABBERLEY, JULIA BLACKMAN PRODUCED BY PAUL WEBSTER, ROBERT LANTOS

R [RESTRICTED]   WRITTEN BY STEVE KNIGHT   COMING SOON   DIRECTED BY DAVID CRONENBERG

FOCUS FEATURES

www.focusfeatures.com/easternpromises

EASTERN PROMISES 2007 (U.K. · CANADA · U.S.)

Director David Cronenberg **Producers** Robert Lantos, Paul Webster
Screenplay Steven Knight **Cinematography** Peter Suschitzky **Music** Howard
Shore **Cast** Vincent Cassel, Viggo Mortensen, Armin Mueller-Stahl, Naomi Watts,
Raza Jaffrey, Radoslaw Kaim, Rhodri Wyn-Miles, Tereza Srbova, Donald Sumpter

Like many gangster films, *Eastern Promises* is about family. But it
is also about the harsh practicalities of immigrant survival. Set
in a grimy London around Christmastime, *Eastern Promises* tells
the almost biblical story of Nikolai (Mortensen) and Anna
(Watts). She is a London nurse of Russian roots who finds the
diary of a dead teenage mother whose infant she takes care of.
He is a factotum for the Vory V Zakone, the Russian Mafia in
London. Anna traces the diary, and the crimes buried inside it,
to the Mafia. Nikolai is instructed to stop her and dispose of
both diary and baby. But he hesitates. Nikolai is actually an
undercover agent, so deeply infiltrated his allegiances have
become blurred, and in Anna he rediscovers the distinction
between right and wrong. His priorities realigned, Nikolai
defeats his bosses and saves Anna and the baby. Nikolai himself,
however, is beyond saving. He has become too much a part of
evil's inner circle. *Eastern Promises* ends with Nikolai as a patriarch
sitting in the Mafia restaurant. He is victorious, but also alone—
emotionally abandoned and physically isolated. The
contemplative resignation of the end reinstates ambiguity into
a story that only seconds before seemed to close happily.

◄

**Filmed in England,
Eastern Promises
was the first
movie that David
Cronenberg shot
entirely away
from Canada. The
gruesome scenes
of violence caused
quite a stir when
it was first released.**

Every single character in *Eastern Promises* has a hyphenated identity, double roots. Steve Knight's screenplay emphasizes the plight of immigrants living in an alienated urban jungle, "a sick city, where it never snows," according to Mafia boss Semyon (Mueller-Stahl). The work of Dostoyevsky too was part of the inspiration. It motivated Cronenberg to create a moody, old-worldly Czarist atmosphere, soaked in sorrow and rituals. Much

"FORGET ANY OF THIS HAPPENED. STAY AWAY FROM PEOPLE LIKE ME."

NIKOLAI

of the story is told through the scars the characters carry, most notably in the tattoos the Mafia members don—in a ceremony full of religious symbolism Nikolai has the stars of Vory V Zakone's leadership tattooed on his body. But it also lies in the genetic imprint of the baby that will implicate the Mafia's crimes, and in the many bruises and injuries of the victims.

That violence attracted a lot of attention. *Eastern Promises* opens with a gruesome throat slitting, and in a notorious bathhouse scene a naked Nikolai is attacked by two leather-clad Chechen heavyweights with scythe-shaped knives. Over the course of three full minutes, Nikolai's nude body is severely cut and beaten, his blood smeared all around the sauna. Nikolai survives by planting a knife straight into the right eye of one of his assailants—a clear wink from Cronenberg to his horror fans that he can still shock us to the core. **EM**

▶
Viggo Mortensen was nominated for Best Actor in recognition of his powerful portrayal of the undercover agent who has infiltrated the Russian Mafia.

MESRINE: KILLER INSTINCT & MESRINE: PUBLIC ENEMY #1 2008 (FRANCE)

Director Jean-François Richet **Producers** Thomas Langmann, André Rouleau, Maxime Rémillard **Screenplay** Abdel Raouf Dafri, Jean-François Richet **Cinematography** Robert Gantz **Music** Marco Beltrami, Marcus Trumpp **Cast** Vincent Cassel, Cécile De France, Gerard Depardieu, Gilles Lelouche, Elena Anya, Ludivine Sagnier, Mathieu Amalric

For almost two decades, Jacques Mesrine enjoyed the notoriety of being France's most infamous criminal. A soldier in Algeria who had witnessed—and was believed to be a participant in—the horrors of war, he became renowned for his daring heists, prison breaks, and even the attempted kidnapping of a judge who had previously sentenced him. He was a maverick among criminals, whose exploits saw him compared to Robin Hood and whose string of glamorous girlfriends gave him celebrity status. His death at the hands of the French police remains shrouded in controversy—less due to surprise that his work would see him dead and more shock at the approach that the French authorities adopted. However, it has helped feed into his near-mythic status. It is perhaps fitting that a biopic of Mesrine's life and incredible exploits should be deemed beyond the scope of one movie, with director Jean-François Richet instead offering a diptych of criminality, charm, and carnage.

The films are bookended by the police operation that resulted in Mesrine's execution on a Parisian street in 1979. From there, Richet offers a relatively linear account of Mesrine's early life, from

◀ The two movies were shot in reverse chronological order so that Vincent Cassel could progressively lose the weight that he gained to play the older Mesrine, as he knew he would not be able to gain weight while filming.

his short stint in the army and his early life as a criminal—halted for a period when he was employed by an architecture firm in an attempt to go straight—to his increasing notoriety as a result of a series of daring criminal exploits.

Though never fully siding with Mesrine and certainly unwilling to shy away from his more violent nature, Richet's films present Mesrine's life with a sheen that recalls the Cinéma du Look in its

> ## "I DON'T LIKE THE LAWS AND I DON'T WANT TO BE A SLAVE OF THE ALARM CLOCK MY WHOLE LIFE." *JACQUES MESRINE*

glossy style. The action is kinetic, taking us through each significant moment in the criminal's chequered and colorful life.

And the numerous set-pieces, from robberies and executions to an audacious prison break, are carried out with aplomb. Richet is aided in no small part by Vincent Cassel's charismatic star turn as the eponymous antihero. Since first attracting international attention in Matthieu Kassovitz's *La Haine* (1995), Cassel has brought a roguish charm to many of his roles. It is to his credit that Cassel draws out the many complexities and contradictions of Mesrine's life and worldview. Though certainly more handsome than the real man, Cassel knowingly balances the aspects of Mesrine's character that made him a cult hero with his rougher edges. He is ably supported by an impressive cast, including Gerard Depardieu, Mathieu Amalric, and Ludivine Sagnier, making *Mesrine* a highly watchable, high-octane true-life thriller. **IHS**

▶ Vincent Cassel was attached to the project for seven years before shooting began, at one point dropping out because he was concerned about making Mesrine look like a hero.

Brad Pitt
killing them softly
CANNES FILM FESTIVAL
OFFICIAL SELECTION
Richard Jenkins James Gandolfini Ray Liotta Scoot McNairy Ben Mendelsohn
PLAN B
ANDREW DOMINIK
KillingThemSoftlyMovie.com

KILLING THEM SOFTLY 2012 (U.S.)

Director Andrew Dominik **Producers** Dede Gardner, Anthony Katagas, Brad Pitt, Paula Mae Schwartz, Steve Schwartz **Screenplay** Andrew Dominik (based on the novel *Cogan's Trade* by George V. Higgins) **Cinematography** Greig Fraser **Cast** Brad Pitt, James Gandolfini, Scoot McNairy, Ben Mendelsohn, Richard Jenkins, Ray Liotta, Sam Shepard

Andrew Dominik's third feature is a brilliant adaptation of George V. Higgins' *Cogan's Trade*. The 1974 novel was Higgins' third to be set in the suburbs of Boston, after *The Friends of Eddie Coyle* (1970, adapted for the screen in 1973 by Peter Yates and starring Robert Mitchum in the titular role) and *The Digger's Game* (1973). Although Boston is mentioned a number of times by characters, the film was actually shot in and around New Orleans. There is a sense that the film is not so much concerned with locale as the state of the whole nation, employing the gangster genre as a microcosm of a country in tatters following 2008's devastating economic meltdown.

Having already swindled his high-stakes poker game once before, Markie Trattman becomes the main suspect when three hooded men hold up another of his games. The heist was actually planned by Johnny "Squirrel" Amato, correctly suspecting that Markie would be fingered for the job. The mob send in Jackie Cogan, a hit man who prefers killing his targets softly, unaware of their impending death. Markie is Cogan's first victim, the hit man believing that a "message" needs to be sent out as a warning. And when Russell, one of the other men who carried

◄

Andrew Dominik was inspired by film noir and screwball comedy studio pictures from the 1940s when casting the movie, wanting each of the characters to be instantly recognizable types from these genres.

out the job, shoots his mouth off about the robbery on a trip to Florida, it doesn't take Cogan long to work out who is responsible.

Following on from the visually ravishing *The Assassination of Jesse James by the Coward Robert Ford* (2007) and his acclaimed debut *Chopper* (2000), Dominik's film an understated crime drama that unfolds at the bottom end of the Mafia structure. There are no heroes and almost all the characters look past their

"I LIKE TO KILL THEM SOFTLY, FROM A DISTANCE. NOT CLOSE ENOUGH FOR FEELINGS." *JACKIE COGAN*

sell-by date. At the center is Brad Pitt's Cogan. It apparently took the director a single text message to convince Pitt to play the mob assassin and the actor delivers one of his best performances. As Markie, Ray Liotta is a bundle of shredded nerves, while Richard Jenkins, James Gandolfini, Ben Mendelsohn, Sam Shepard, and Scoot McNairy all add color to their characters.

▶
Much of the movie takes place in cars. Brad Pitt described it as "a big challenge to make a scene last for nine minutes when it's just two characters talking in a car."

What makes the film so vital is the fact that Dominik has located Higgins' novel specifically during the lead-up to the 2008 U.S. presidential election. In doing so he equates the mafia's business affairs with the disastrous state of the country's economy. It is a powerful indictment of greed and an ethos that has brought a nation to its knees. But Cogan may be one step ahead of the future president in identifying the problem. In one of the film's final scenes, as Obama is seen making a speech on TV, Cogan states, "America's not a country ... It's just a business." **IHS**

INDEX